THE ART OF CHRISTIAN LIVING

THE ART OF CHRISTIAN LIVING

Christian Faith and Mental Health

Ralph Heynen

BAKER BOOK HOUSE
Grand Rapids, Michigan

To
      Ida
and our four daughters,
who have been a great source
of inspiration and encouragement.

Preface

Near Grand Rapids, Michigan, on a spacious campus, beautifully landscaped with lofty Pine trees, is a unique Christian mental hospital. Established and supported by members of the various Reformed churches, it has been a haven of healing for more than half a century. It is founded on the basic concept that there is a close relationship between Christian faith and mental health.

In this hospital, the best and latest in scientific means of healing are blended with the Calvinistic view of life. Psychiatrists, psychologists, social workers, nurses and therapists work hand in hand with pastors to provide healing and strength to those suffering from emotional and mental illnesses. It is a living proof of the theory that man is an organic unity, in whom body, mind and spirit are intimately interwined.

Christian faith has always played an important role in emotional stability. A man with a strong and vibrant trust in God will move through life with steadfastness of goal and purpose. He will have a source of strength available in his daily activities and in the hours of crisis.

The chapters of this book have grown out of two decades of experience as chaplain of this Christian mental hospital. They first appeared as weekly articles in *The Banner,* a church periodical, published by the Christian Reformed Publishing House. It is with the gracious permission of the Board of Publication and the encouragement of Christian friends that some of these articles are assembled in the present form.

The aim of this volume is to show that mental health is more than the absence of distressing symptoms in the mental and emotional life. It is a positive state of well-being in a person who is adjusted to the physical, mental and spiritual factors within himself. It reveals a person who has come to terms with himself, with others, with his environment and with his God.

This rests on the implication that faith must enter into every fibre of a man's personality. It brings a unifying, strengthening and developing force in man. A life dominated by a faith that can fully express itself through the emotional and mental resources within is one that can accept frustrations, disappointments and defeats with serenity of spirit.

This volume is presented with a prayer that the Holy Spirit, who only can implant and strengthen our faith, will use it to lead others to a deeper Christian faith and to better mental health.

RALPH HEYNEN

Contents

INTRODUCTION

1. Think on These Things............................. 13
2. The Color of Our Thoughts........................ 15

BASIC CONCEPTS OF MENTAL HEALTH

3. The Influence of the Mind on the Body.............. 19
4. Soul and Body.................................... 23
5. Living with Ourselves............................. 25
6. The Tyranny of Things............................ 27
7. Adaptability 30
8. The Soul Looks Up............................... 33

LEARNING TO CONQUER OURSELVES

9. Learning Self-control 37
10. Learning from Our Critics........................ 40
11. Too Much of Self................................ 43
12. Faultfinding 46
13. Inconsistencies 49
14. Prejudice 52
15. Let's Stop Pretending............................ 54
16. Anger 57
17. Developing Self-confidence 60

QUALITIES OF CHRISTIAN CHARACTER

18. A Cheerful Heart Is a Good Medicine................ 65
19. Can You See Straight?............................ 68
20. Learning to Relax................................ 70
21. The Cost of Pride................................ 72
22. The Cost of Friendship............................ 74
23. Inlet and Outlet................................. 76
24. The Art of Forgetting............................. 79
25. The Chambers of Imagery......................... 82
26. When We Stand Alone............................ 84
27. Patience — A Dynamic Virtue...................... 86

LIVING WITH OUR EMOTIONS

28. That Tired Feeling.................................... 91
29. Feelings of Guilt..................................... 94
30. Feelings of Loneliness................................ 97
31. Don't Step on My Toes............................... 99
32. Overcoming Jealousy 101
33. Our Hidden Resentments............................ 104
34. Depression 106
35. Your Nerves and You................................ 109
36. Accentuating Our Successes.......................... 111

HANDLING OUR TENSIONS AND ANXIETIES

37. Living in a Time of Tension.......................... 115
38. Conflicting Desires 118
39. Tension — Your Master, or Your Servant...............121
40. Common-sense Remedies for Tension.................. 123
41. What Is Anxiety..................................... 125
42. Our Anxieties and Our Faith......................... 127
43. Flight or Fight...................................... 129
44. Learn to Conquer Worry............................. 132
45. Being Driven by the Clock........................... 135
46. The Search for Security.............................. 137

DEVELOPING A SENSE OF VALUES

47. Aimless Living 143
48. Our Sense of Values................................. 146
49. Our Needs and Our Wants............................ 148
50. Making Decisions 150
51. The Frustrated Perfectionist......................... 153

TOWARDS EMOTIONAL AND SPIRITUAL MATURITY

52. The Perils of Pessimism.............................. 157
53. How Old Are You?................................... 159
54. Putting Away Childish Things........................ 161
55. How Mature Are We?................................ 163
56. Those Twenty Added Years........................... 166
57. The Fear of Growing Old............................. 168
58. The Power of Hope.................................. 170

INTRODUCTION

Finally brethren, whatsoever things are true,
whatsoever things are honorable,
whatsoever things are just,
whatsoever things are pure,
whatsoever things are lovely,
whatsoever things are of good report;
if there be any virtue, and if there be any praise,
think on these things.
........these things do:
and the God of peace shall be with you.

— St. Paul, in Philippians 4:8, 9

1. Think on These Things

The realm of our thoughts is a most fascinating one. It is one of the greatest gifts of a bountiful Creator. The operation of millions of tiny cells in the human brain lifts man into a sphere where he stands alone among the creatures — in his ability to think.

Our thoughts can transport us to places where we have never been. They are a magic carpet that can bring back the experiences of the past or the great scenes of history. By them we visit the Garden of Eden, or Rome in the days of her glory.

This fascinating power also brings us in touch with the Eternal, for here we share in the likeness of Him whose image we bear. How it enriches our lives! What marvels it unfolds and what beauties it holds!

But the mind can also be an area of life that is filled with terrors, possibly more so than any other area of life. It oftens calls up fears, both real and imaginary. It musters up moments of great anxiety and days of troublesome worries. Here often lie lodged deep hostilities that make life miserable and that can incapacitate the person. There are also illnesses of the mind that call up horrible phantasms and ghostly images. It can become an instrument that produces great pain and distress.

POWER OF THOUGHT

The powers of our thoughts can be a tremendous influence for good. Thoughts are the materials with which we work. Before any great deed is done, it is conceived in the mental life. Before a large building is constructed it has first been seen in the mind of an architect. Before a great institution is born it is fashioned in the hopes and dreams of its founders. Thoughts are important, for, "as a man thinketh, so he is."

This is true also for evil. Before we commit a sin, we have first had a sinful thought. Before we tell a lie we have thought one. Before we speak a profane word, we have had a profane thought.

There are also many thoughts that never come to expression in overt acts. There are hostilities, envies, and impurities in our thoughts that are never openly expressed, but they are sins. We shall also be judged for our thoughts.

This leads to the conclusion that the mental life is extremely important for the Christian. It is an area of life that must be brought more and more under the sway of the redemptive work of Christ in us. Here lies the great need for a Christian Mental Health.

A CHRISTIAN MENTAL HEALTH

Physical health is the complete and successful functioning of every part of the human being in harmonious relationship with every other part and with its environment. Mental health depends also upon our measure of adjustment to our surroundings. A healthy man is one who is in harmony with himself, with his fellow-men and with his environment. There is co-ordination and balance in his life.

We are convinced that there is also a Christian Mental Health. The Bible and the Christian faith have something positive to say about a healthy mind. I would contend also that this holds not only for the mental health of the Christian but also for a Christian Mental Health.

It is our plan to suggest certain things which the Christian faith can contribute to Mental health. We may be Christians and yet lack the wholeness of mind which we should have. There are avenues of faith which we should travel which will help us to have a better balanced view of life.

Naturally, my view will be colored by experiences in dealing with those who have to a greater or lesser degree lost their mental equilibrium. But possibly this background can give us certain insights that will be helpful to understand this mysterious yet fascinating field.

Christian Mental Health must always be based on the Bible and the teachings of the Christian faith. Of this we have a beautiful example in the words of Paul, "Think on These Things." Think on the things that are true, honest, just, pure, lovely and of good report. This is positive thinking at its best. But lest the Christian should become a mystic dreamer he adds, "these things do; and the God of peace shall be with you."

2. The Color of Our Thoughts

The psychology of color is a wide and complex field. Some colors are warm, others are cold; some are cheerful, others are somber. There are certain shades of blue which we would never think of using in our hospital rooms. We would never think of dressing a nurse in a bright red uniform. Such colors would have a disturbing effect.

Common usage also expresses the fact that color influences our human spirit. A person is said to be blue when he is depressed or sad. We describe others as being green with envy. The coward is said to be yellow, the anarchist is red, white is associated with purity.

Marcus Aurelius, a Roman philosopher, reminds us that, "The soul is dyed the color of its thoughts." There is a color to our thoughts.

SOMBER THOUGHTS

There are some people I know whose thoughts must be a sort of somber grey. Whenever they talk about anything they tend to bring out the gloomy side of life. They can tell about all the recent accidents, the people who have cancer, and all the funerals. Their thoughts seem to flow in a gloomy mood. They have usually lost their sense of humor.

Others have thoughts that are perennially tinged in green. They are envious and jealous of others. They have suspicions about all people who prosper. They rarely have a good word to say for others because they see them through eyes that are green with covetousness.

When you hear the conversation of others, you cannot help but feel that their minds must be veritable cesspools. Sordid stories, profane remarks, suggestive statements flow from their lips. Such minds are filled with filth. I often feel sorry for people who must listen to them.

Others tinge their thoughts with varying shades of blue. Their minds are full of worries, anxieties and fears. They see the road of life ahead of them and at every fork of the way they are sure that things are going to go wrong. They see dangers before them and threatenings behind them, and they always find new grounds for grave concern. They are anxious about many things, most of which will never happen.

FURNISHINGS OF THE MIND

But what about the color of our thoughts? You can determine their color, for it depends entirely on what you put into your mind. When people fill their minds with drab and lowly things, the furnishings of the chamber of the mind will be drab. But when we fill them with rich and noble thoughts, the chamber of the mind will be richly furnished.

When people fill their minds with that which they read in the papers and magazines, or the things seen on TV, or when the mind is filled only with the material aspects of life, the color of the mind will be somber and gloomy. For when God created the mental power of man, He intended that it should have both a horizontal and a vertical aspect. Man was not made to live by bread alone.

For the Christian there must be infinitely more. He fills his mind with the noble and the lofty things of life. The reading of great books; listening to the strains of great music; seeing the beauties of nature and art; or exploring the wonders of science—all these—but in all he sees at each turning of the way that God is there, God in His greatness, and God in His love.

This we need, for the "soul is dyed the color of its thoughts." It is only in fellowship with Him that our thoughts are ennobled and enriched. We must learn to pray, "Search me, O God, and know my thoughts" and "Let the meditations of our hearts be acceptable in Thy sight."

PLACE OF FAITH

By thinking in terms of faith in Christ our whole life will be colored by it. For when the soul is washed "whiter than the snow" so also our mind will be. And it will be filled with the rosy optimism of the Christian, not based on the illusive spirit of the age, but in the knowledge that He who holds the world in His hand will lead all things to His own purposes and goals.

Furnish then the chambers of the mind with these ennobling, cleansing, reverent thoughts, and all of life will share in the rays of its light. It is like standing on the shore of a lake at sunset. When the sun slips beyond the horizon it sends its rays of scarlet and pink and purple through all the sky, but also the waters of the lake will be tinged by these brilliant hues. So will our lives be when our thoughts are colored by the light that shines from Him who is the *Sun of Righteousness*.

BASIC CONCEPTS OF MENTAL HEALTH

What is man,
that Thou art mindful of him?
And the son of man,
that Thou visitest him?
For Thou hast made him a little lower
than the angels,
and hast crowned him with glory and honor.
Thou madest him to have dominion
over the works of Thy hands.
O Lord our Lord,
How excellent is Thy name in all the earth.

— David, in Psalm 8

3. The Influence of the Mind on the Body

Doctors tell us that a large percentage of the patients who come to them with physical complaints actually have emotional problems that undermine their health. Many people who do have physical sicknesses have a hard time getting well again because they have such an unhealthy attitude towards their illness and towards life in general.

In recent years a great deal of stress has been laid upon the subject of psychosomatic medicine. This stresses the close relationship between the psychical and the physical, the mind and the body. For the human personality is a unity. Body and soul are two elements of the same person, and they are intimately intertwined in their work.

We are all familiar with the deep sense of power that flows from a man or woman who lives on a lofty mental and spiritual level. The inner strength is also reflected in the functioning of the body. There is a composure in the way the person carries himself that reflects a sense of serene confidence within.

On the other hand, we know persons who are physically strangely ineffective because of mental and emotional weakness. The body often affects the mind and emotions but it is even more true that the mind and the feelings have a tremendous influence over the body.

BIBLICAL LANGUAGE

In the days when the Bible was written, the emotional functions were often described in physical terms. There is reference to the "bowels of mercy," for it was commonly thought that the spirit of compassion was located in the intestinal tract. The kidneys were considered to have a great influence upon desire and longing. The King James version rather discreetly speaks of the "reins," but other versions translate it more accurately as the "kidneys." The term "heart" is also used often in Scripture. The heart is considered to be the very center of life, the very wellspring of emotional and spiritual life. It is stated, "Out of the heart are the issues of life." These are figures of speech, but they indicate some of the common conceptions of the day.

In fact, we do the same today. The figures of modern speech indicate that we feel that the mind influences the body. We speak of a person that annoys us as "getting under our skin." The people whom we resent a great deal give us a "pain in the neck." Others "make us sick." We hear something that thrills us, such as a beautiful piece of music, and it "sends chills up and down our spine." The scratching of a finger nail on a black-board "gives us a chill," and something that we find very disgusting is said to "turn our stomach."

These are more than metaphors and figures of speech. They are actual factors with which we live. They indicate the strange power the mind has over the body.

PHYSICAL SYMPTOMS

Often people with emotional problems have difficulties with their skin. It is not uncommon to see rashes, hives and eczema that have an emotional basis. These are skin lesions that usually do not respond to medicine, but that do respond to release from the tensions and anxieties that cause them. Such people have literally allowed certain mental factors to get under their skin.

It is common knowledge that peptic ulcers are frequently found in people living under tension. Such people tend to drive themselves, and possibly others who work with and for them, beyond that which is good for them.

Emotional tensions can also express themselves in headaches and aches in various parts of the body, such as a pain in the neck. Extreme anger and hostility can create exhaustion and chronic fatigue.

In fact, all strong emotions are accompanied with bodily reactions. When we have sorrow, we weep; when we are joyful, we laugh; when we are ashamed, we blush; when we have fear, the heart beats faster and the rate of breathing increases, and in extreme cases the blood pressure may rise.

The most extreme example of the power of the mind over the body can be seen in persons who are under the spell of a neurosis. There are those who become paralyzed, so that they cannot walk, or even move their arms. This is then not due to any physical cause, but to their emotional state.

HEALTH IS WHOLENESS

If it is true that the body is influenced by the inner self in a negative way, it is also true in a positive way. If our emotional and mental attitudes can make us miserable or sick, they can also lead us to a greater degree of health. We cannot expect good physical health if we have poor mental health; the two are closely inter-related.

Jesus often used the term "that they may be made whole." True health requires the kind of "wholeness" in which every part of man works together as an integrated whole. It requires that all the factors that go into life form a harmonious unity.

To be really healthy we need healthy emotions, healthy thoughts and healthy values in life as well as a good heart and an efficient digestive system. Here lies the ground work for constructive living.

Peace of mind, contentment and serenity of spirit are reflected in the quiet and orderly working of the body. Digestion is aided when there is a pleasant spirit around the dinner table. When love dominates the mind and the warm glow of tenderness, happiness and sympathy are found in the heart, the physical mechanisms will function more properly.

The lighter side of life—laughter, recreation and play—are also important for our physical well-being. Beauty too has its place in the pattern of wholeness that is good for the entire self.

The person that worries so much that he cannot sleep at night will, as a rule, suffer for it the next day also. Fatigue can often be caused by insomnia. The man or woman, boy or girl, who at the close of the day can kneel before his God, confess his sins, and then rest in the confidence that he has a loving Father in heaven, can find peaceful sleep. This is a mark of both health and wholeness.

The attitude of reverence and worship have a wholesome effect upon the activities of the entire week. The quietness of heart that a serene and trusting spirit brings can also lead to better health.

For what our Lord said to the man with the palsy is really true: "Thy Faith has made Thee whole."

4. Soul and Body

A very familiar phrase that is often uttered is, "If people were only born-again Christians they would not have these emotional problems." Others express this thought a bit more modestly when they say, "I feel that if I had a stronger faith, I would not have this problem."

This is a common idea, but it rests on the mistake of making a separation between soul and body, between the spiritual and the physical. It tends to divide man into various segments. It is important to uphold the organic unity of the personality.

DEFINING PERSONALITY

It is not easy to come to a clear-cut definition of personality. The Christian Association for Psychological Studies, an organization of Christian professional people interested in the study of psychology, has spent several sessions in a study of this subject. I have no intention of solving this question in a brief article.

So much depends on our viewpoint. We must always emphasize the truth of the image of God in man. Since God is the supreme Person, we are personalities only because we bear his image and likeness.

One thought that seems to stand out clearly is that there is an inner self that expresses itself in the various relationships of life. In a healthy person these relationships are integrated in a harmonious way. If this balance is missing, we have a person who lacks mental health.

THE INNER SELF

There is an inner core of the person which we may call the inner "I." This center of life expresses itself in all we do, say, or think. We say, "I walk," "I think," "I love" or "I believe," and it is always the same "I."

This central core of personality is well-nigh indefinable. We can never quite know it, because it lives in the unconscious. We know it is there, but we cannot touch it. This is indeed the Holy of Holies in us. It is the most important element in man, and yet it dwells in mystic seclusion. Out of it are all the issues of life.

It is here that God carries on his work in us. It is here that the Spirit of God dwells as He enters at our regeneration. I like to describe this as the inner man.

VARIOUS DIMENSIONS

This inner core of the personality expresses itself in various directions. We commonly describe four dimensions. A simple and useful description is given in the following terms:

1. *The "I - Me" relationship.* The inner man must express itself in our own personal life. This includes the interworking of soul and body, of the feelings and the intellect, between the physical and the spiritual.

Modern medicine has shown that the inner self exerts a tremendous power over the body. Many of our illnesses flow from the influence of the mind, or the feelings, upon our physical life. In this respect a man may be at war with himself, or he may be at peace with himself.

When this aspect of life is over-emphasized the life of man becomes too self-centered or selfish. Each person must come to terms with himself.

2. *The "I - It" relationship.* We also stand in relationship to our environment, with the world in which we live. This may be the tools with which we work, the house in which we live, or the street on which we live. Each person must come to grips with his environs.

When this relationship becomes the highest in man, he becomes a materialist.

3. *The "I - We" relationship.* The inner man also reaches out through various avenues to other people. This begins when we are children and we feel our dependency upon our mothers. It further develops in the family, in the community, in the church and the world.

It is the same "I" that must come to grips with social environment, with the people with whom we live, work or worship.

4. *The "I - Thou" relationship.* The inner "I" also enters into relationship with God. Man feels his dependence upon his Maker, and his soul is restless until it finds rest in him. It is in this relationship that man reaches his highest, for as a person he can taste fellowship with a personal God.

A BALANCED VIEWPOINT

We believe that God carries on his work in the inner man. His work of regeneration takes place in the heart, in the very core of man's being. From the inner citadel of the soul man expresses himself in all of life's relationships.

If there is a lack of balance in any or several of these various dimensions of his person, we cannot therefore conclude that such a person is not born again. There may be some defect or illness in the person that does not allow him to express his new nature in some of these relationships of his life.

I know people, whom I consider to be sincere Christians, but who have difficulty in their personal life, their social life and even their spiritual life. Somewhere along the line there is a breakdown in the person so that they are not able to give adequate expression to the inner man.

Naturally, this does not answer all the questions. I would like to develop this thought in a few succeeding chapters. But this view of man does show the great importance of the soul. The Bible also teaches this fact.

Satan knows the importance of your soul and mine, for he seeks it. The angels know it, for they rejoice over one soul that is saved. Jesus knew it, and gave his life to ransom the soul. Can you also say, "It is well with my soul"?

5. Living with Ourselves

There are some people who are hard to get along with. They have traits of character that make it unpleasant to be with them. They suffer from what one writer describes as "personality halitosis." Usually we try to spend as little time as possible with them. But the fact remains that such people do have to live with themselves twenty-four hours a day.

A person with a hot temper does not make a pleasant companion, but have you ever thought how hard it must be for such a person to live with himself? A person with a jealous disposition does not make a good friend, but such a person must live with that disposition all the time.

It is a good thing to examine our own lives to see what kind of persons we are really living with. For we must all live with ourselves.

INTROSPECTION

In our modern world we tend to look about us a good deal, and the horizons of life are constantly widening. But in this process we have lost the fine art of introspection. We often think that the process of looking within is only practiced by people who have withdrawn from the busy stream of life. But it is an art that we should all learn.

THE "I - ME" RELATIONSHIP

In our previous chapter we tried to show that the inner core of our personality expresses itself in four relationships. The first of these is the relationship to ourselves. There are certain delicate balances within us. We should look well to these inner relationships. We must keep a balance between the emotional and the mental, between the physical and the spiritual, and between the old nature and the new.

I suppose all of us have tried at some time to take one of these personality tests which appear in popular magazines. I know, we all cheat a little bit in taking them because we mark them in our own favor. These tests are a good beginning in examining our inner selves. They tell us a good deal about ourselves, especially if we face them honestly.

LOOKING WITHIN

But more than that, we should spend some time each day in

reflection. We should examine our life to see what kind of person we are. Ask yourself the question, "Am I the kind of person I would like to live with the rest of my life?"

It is unfortunate that many of us spend so little time in reflection, until in the providence of God we are forced into it by some personal crisis. When we are laid aside for a time of illness, or when we face some great problem, we must begin to do some introspective thinking. Sessions in counseling and psychotherapy require a great deal of soul searching.

I am sure that every person is capable of some kind of reflectiveness. It is good for us to meet ourselves as we really are in the depth of our being. This is always the first step in character and personality growth. It is not learned in an hour, or a day, or even a year. It requires a lifetime. But it is essential for real growth.

A DEEPER UNDERSTANDING

Practical psychology can be of great help in learning to know ourselves. But there is something deeper which is experienced in spiritual introspection. It is the understanding that comes to us when we place ourselves in the presence of God and pray, "Search me, O God, and know my heart; try me, and know my thought."

There is no better way to learn to know yourself than to be alone with God. In the inner chamber there is no room for sham and hypocrisy, for we are well aware that an all-seeing eye is present. The external façade of the person fades away there. In this attitude of heart we begin to know ourselves in depth.

Too often in such moments of reflection we still remain in generalities. Many people will be more than ready to admit that all is not well, that they are sinners. But if you should ask them to mention 10 of these sins they would not be able to do it. But we don't really know ourselves until we can identify the dominant sins of our life.

All this leads to one conclusion. Living with ourselves requires that we live as in the presence of God. For in the light of his presence we see our sins and failings, but also experience the joy of his forgiving love. The real victory over the weaknesses and sins in ourselves is found in the Christ. "We are more than conquerors through him that loved us."

6. The Tyranny of Things

Each one of us lives in a world of things. From morning till evening we are surrounded by various objects with which we come in contact. No man can escape them, even if he wanted to. The bed in which we sleep, the clothes we wear, the home in which we live, the food we eat, the tools with which we work, the cars we drive and the trees with all their brilliant hues are all a part of our environment.

Each one of us must come to terms with his own environment. To a certain extent we make our own environment, in another way it is made for us. We can choose certain aspects of the world about us, but much of it is thrust upon us, whether we like it or not.

This points out the "I - It" relationship of which we wrote in an earlier chapter.

OUR EARLY ENVIRONMENT

In early development in children the surroundings do play a considerable role. A child born in a slum area in one of our large cities will have certain difficulties to overcome. It does make a difference to us in our formative years, whether we are born in an urban community or a rural area. If one comes from a home where there is considerable wealth there will be a different outlook upon the external world than if one is born in a home where there is poverty.

I do not feel, however, that these factors are final determinants. For we know that leading men in the field of politics and science have been born on the wrong side of the tracks, and that some of our best known criminals come from homes where wealth and culture abounded.

Basically, it depends on the attitudes we assume to the world about us. We must come to terms with our environment.

ABSORBED WITH THINGS

One of the characteristics of our modern society is the fact that we are overly much concerned about things. This material environment of ours plays a tremendous role in the lives of most of us. There are thousands, if not millions, of people who are more interested in making a living than in making a life. The only purpose for their daily work is to provide food, clothing and shelter for their family and themselves. Their primary concern in life is the pay check that comes every other Friday, and the things it will buy for them.

This is equally true among those who have a good deal of this world's goods, and among those who have little. The difference may be that one is concerned about how to pay his bills, while the other is more concerned about the ebb and flow of the stock market. But material things form the chief place in heart and mind.

Others are forever worrying about things. Their anxieties move in the world of the material rather than of the spiritual. These are materialists, and the god of things is worshiped much more in this world of ours than the God in heaven.

DRIVEN BY A DESIRE FOR THINGS

In this highly commercialized society there is much that is offered for sale. You are urged to buy, for you can always get it on easy credit terms. You can mortgage your own future just to have the satisfaction of possession. For, the real mark of success is to have many things that the world counts to be important.

Unconsciously all of us have a desire to possess fully as much as our friends have, and if possible, a little more. You can build some marvelous dreams with a mail-order catalogue, especially in the days of youth. This spirit has taken hold of us to a far greater extent than we often realize.

The result of this is a restless striving for things, a yearning that can never be fully satisfied; for, the more we have, the more we will want. It leads to a spirit of discontent that is most unhealthy — emotionally, mentally and spiritually. We have come to live under the tyranny of things. We have allowed the material world to dominate us, rather than, as God intended, that we rule over the world of the material that surrounds us.

LEARNING CONTENTMENT

Evidently this materialistic spirit has been with us a long time. The Bible speaks out against it in no uncertain terms. Rich King Solomon says, "Give me neither riches nor poverty; feed me with the food that is needful for me." The Apostle Paul displays a marvelous spirit of detachment from the material world when he says, "I have learned in whatsoever state I am, therein to be content. I know how to be abased, and I know also how to abound." He had been unspoiled in days of prosperity and unbroken by adversity.

This is good mental health, for it is an expression of satisfaction in the midst of the appropriate environment. But it is a spirit that is a bit scarce, even among our people.

Many of those who have the Midas touch are most unhappy people, for there are things you cannot buy. There are others who have little but who spend themselves vainly to "gain the world." I am sure that this is one of the most common subjects for worry, one of the most frequent sources of family quarrels, one of the most common causes for envy and distrust, and one of the prime reasons for emotional tensions and breakdown.

In the "I - It" relationship of life, when the inner self reaches out to the world about us, do not allow yourself to come under the tyranny of things. For the material world may not be a blind that hides God from our view, but it must be a window through which we see our God. It must be a stepping stone on which we stand to look ahead and beyond.

7. Adaptability

At a recent pastors' conference a minister described one of his parishioners. "He is the kind of man for whom there are only two sides to any question, the one he holds, and the wrong one." There are such people. I am sure that we all know one or two of them. They are so sure of their own viewpoint that they can see no other.

There is nothing so obnoxious as a person who thinks that he is always right, who never compromises, and who is happy when he can assert his own ideas in an argument. Some people may describe them as men of conviction, others will say that they are just plain stubborn. I suppose it depends on whether you agree with them or not.

Such people have a low level of adaptability.

RIGID THOUGHT PATTERNS

In our personal relationships with others we need a good deal of flexibility. When two people meet there are bound to be differences, for no two people will ever think exactly alike on every issue. It is only normal for a husband and wife to have their differences, for children to differ with their parents, because each person has a right to his own opinions.

It is hard to live with a person who has extremely rigid thought patterns. Usually, rigidity of thinking is considered to be the mark of a strong personality. But actually, such attitudes towards others betrays an inner weakness, a feeling of insecurity. Such a person does not really dare to look at the other side of the issue.

The person who has nothing to feel threatened about in his dealings with others is not afraid to admit that he may be wrong and that there may be other sides to the question. He does not go around with a chip on his shoulder trying to defend his own viewpoint, but he feels that his views will stand on their own merit.

NARROW-MINDEDNESS

During a Presidential campaign we hear a lot of people speak with almost fanatical devotion to their own party. They have closed their minds to the fact that the other party may also have some good points, and that their own party may have a few weak spots.

Some people take this same view when it comes to the church. They feel that there is just one side to the question, and they prefer not to hear the other side. There is a tendency to classify people into two categories, either they are "with us" or they are "outsiders."

It always reminds me of the somewhat paranoid feelings of the Romans and the Greeks who considered all who were not of their own culture to be "barbarians."

In such a view of life the "I - We" relationship has weakened. It has become "I - we" instead of "I - We." There is too much "I" and too little "We."

BALANCED VIEWPOINT

We should try to keep the boat of life in balance, for if we shift our weight too much to one side or to the other we are liable to tip. We must not slip into the error of never having an idea of our own. A person who always agrees with you is a very poor friend. It is hard to converse with him, because there is little interplay of ideas and exchange of thought.

We need people who think for themselves. But we need a balance between the two extremes. The rigid person is in danger of intolerance and even bigotry. But the man who tries to be agreeable to everyone that comes along is liable to be a weak and spineless personality.

We need convictions upon which we can build our lives; we need standards by which we can live, but we must be willing to give and take on those matters of life that are not of great consequence. I am sure that you will agree that many of the differences in our homes, between parents and children, and even between members of a church, are not caused by matters of conviction, but by the little things that could well have been reconciled, if we were a bit more adaptable.

PAUL'S VIEW OF LIFE

None of us would consider the Apostle Paul as a man who could be easily swept along with the tide. He tells us "I am become all things to all men, that I may by all means save some." These words are sometimes applied unfavorably to people, especially to ministers. When it is said of them that "they are all things to all men" it is by no means intended as a compliment.

But Paul had learned to be at home in all classes of society. He had not gained this by reading *How to Win Friends and Influence People,* but he had learned this as a gift of grace, although I believe it was also a part of his native character.

He was a man of versatile sympathies. For, effective Christian living requires adaptability. We must learn to understand others and practice that understanding. We must learn to enter into the heart and life of others.

It depends upon the goal we have in mind. Paul's goal, "that I may win some," was a lofty one. We need the same goal in our lives. There is danger that we possibly may be more interested in tradition than in saving others. We may be critical rather than seeking to help others.

We may not sacrifice convictions for expediency, but we must learn to yield in a thousand little things so that we may be able to accomplish the great things of life. This involves humility and self-suppression. But it is worth it, if we may perchance win some.

Adaptability is a Christian virtue. Let's practice it.

8. The Soul Looks Up

We have been thinking about the various relationships of life as expressed in the terms "I-Me," "I-It," and "I-We." The most important of these relationships is expressed in terms of "I-Thou," for here the soul looks up to God.

It is also a relationship that can cause problems in a person's emotional life, for basically, our emotions play a great role in our spiritual life. We would like to look at the relationship between the soul and God especially in the light of the question so frequently asked, "If I had a stronger faith, would I still have these emotional struggles and problems?"

IS THERE A RELIGIOUS INSTINCT?

A number of psychologists place the spiritual desires of man among the instinctive drives. It is common for all people to cling to some higher power, "somebody bigger than you or I." This upward surge of the inner man is then described as the religious instinct in man. It is placed alongside of various other drives.

Psychologically this may or may not be sound, depending to a large extent on the definition of "instinct." But from a Scriptural standpoint this offers a very shallow view of the religious nature of man. It is far removed from the words of Augustine, "The soul is restless until it finds rest in Thee."

The true beginnings of the spiritual desires in man lie in the image of God. For the inner self, or the soul, is the most important part of our personality. And yet, it is also the most mysterious. It is the holy of holies within us, where no man can tread, and which none can fully know.

It is here that God enters with his Spirit and with his regenerating powers. This brings a radical change in the inner man. For, while we were "dead in trepasses and sins," now we are "made alive again" by the spiritual rebirth. From this changed inner self flows the true "I-Thou" relationship.

DIFFERENCES IN RELIGIOUS OUTLOOK

Even though it is the same Spirit that regenerates every Christian, there are still vast differences in their spiritual outlook. For some the Christian faith is a joyous and happy experience, others more of the gloomy side. Someone has observed that in the choir of God there is a place for the sopranos and tenors as well as for the altos and basses. There was room for both Peter and Thomas in the apostolic circle.

Generally, the Reformed faith would be classified among th authoritarian religion. Calvinism is often identified with a stern outlook upon life, and a rather rigid emphasis. It would seem to me that this is not true to the basic principles of the Reformed faith. There has always been room for a rather wide divergence of feelings as well as viewpoints. That is one of the things I like about Calvinism.

The differences in religious outlook depend a great deal on the concept we have of God. If we constantly picture God as a stern and angry Father, and then possibly identify him with a stern and rigid earthly father, we are going to come up with a gloomy outlook on religion, with a great deal of emphasis on sin and guilt and a minimum of emphasis on forgiveness and grace.

If however, we look up to a God of love and compassion, one who comes with the smile of forgiveness, who holds out lofty ideals and hopes for his children, we will be able to see more of the glory of our relationship with God.

A BALANCED OUTLOOK

We need a view of the loftiness, the sovereignty and the power Calvary, for He is one. We must, as Christians who have felt the regenerating powers of the Holy Spirit, look out also to the Father of our Lord Jesus Christ.

We need a view of the loftiness, the sovereignty and the power of God, but we must also know him as a God who is love. It may seem a bit trite to say this, but in my experience with many with emotional problems, I find that there is often an unreal or an un balanced view of God.

For, our concept of God will also color our whole outlook on life. We cannot, even if we would want to, dissociate our religious outlook from our emotional outlook. For, the whole structure of man is involved in the spiritual life.

In dealing with people who tend to have depressed thoughts, who are inclined to see the gloomy side of life rather than the bright side, I find that the spiritual outlook is always involved. People with a very rigid view of life, unbending in their relationship with others, will show this attitude also in their religious life. Religion forms a part of the whole web of life, it is not just a few strands that are interwoven.

The Scripture presents us with a marvelous picture of God. We see him there in the loftiness of his being and also in the tenderness of his love. But the great question for each of us is, "What is the vision that we have of him?" What does our soul see when it looks up?

LEARNING TO CONQUER OURSELVES

For though we walk in the flesh,
we do not war according to the flesh;
For the weapons of our warfare are not of the flesh,
but mighty before God
to the casting down of strongholds;
Casting down imaginations,
and every high thing that is exalted against the
knowledge of God,
and bringing every thought into captivity
to the obedience of Christ.

— St. Paul, in II Corinthians 10:3-5

9. Learning Self-control

An automobile out of control is a dangerous bit of equipment on our highways. A fire burning out of control leads to great destruction of property. But even more tragic and dangerous is the life of a man out of control. Some of the tragic pages which have been written in history have to do with people who had not learned to control themselves.

Alexander the Great had practically conquered the world, but he lost his temper and killed one of his best generals and most trusted friends. Peter the Great confessed, "I have conquered an empire, but I have not been able to control myself." A moment of lack of self-control cost Moses the right to enter the promised land.

The examples could be multiplied a thousandfold, for today there are tragedies in many homes due to lack of self-control on the part of some member of the family. Many communities have been sadly disrupted by the lack of this important quality in the leaders or members of such a community. Many people have broken their health of body and mind by the absence of true restraint.

One of the admirable traits of President Abraham Lincoln was the art of bringing feelings under rigid discipline. Lincoln was perhaps the most criticized and maligned president ruling in a critical hour of history, but he could keep the nation under control since he was able to keep himself under control.

FRUSTRATIONS IN LIFE

Life is full of frustrating experiences; all of us have them at times. There are minor ones, such as the things people say about us that we do not like, or the frustrations we encounter when we are driving in heavy traffic. We are often provoked, and resentments stir up within us, or we may even be moved to anger.

Then there are also larger and more far-reaching experiences that cause wounds and try our souls. Long periods of illness, the loss of a loved one, or the disappointments that come to us through our business or work — these also leave their scars in our emotional life. They can cause grief, resentment or inner pain.

REPRESSION

One way that is often used to meet these frustrations is to repress these feelings. We try to press them into the background of our subconscious life. We may be angry at someone, but it is not nice to show anger, so we allow it to fester in our hearts. We say, "I'll just forget about it this time, but if it ever happens again, I'll get even somehow."

Such repressions of feeling are not healthy. The sore remains even though we try to salve it over; we have merely hidden it. The anger is still there — we have only buried it for awhile. When a more convenient time comes, it will again boil over, and we will express it far more violently than before.

Some people treat sin and guilt this way, too. When a sin is committed at first it seems rather fresh in the mind and conscience. But, if it is not humbly confessed, and the blessing of forgiveness found, it lies dormant and buried. Often this is the basis of disquietude of heart in a sensitive person. It may even contribute to emotional breakdowns.

Repression is the failure to face up to the reality of our inner feelings. This does not lead to proper self-control. Many resentments have their beginnings in this way, and they continue to fester in the life of a person, and break out repeatedly in various forms.

STEPS TO SELF-CONTROL

There is a better way to get ourselves under control. It is like a stairway with several steps, and the climb is not an easy one. But there is a real satisfaction when we reach the top. The discipline of the soul is never easy, but it is always worthwhile.

First of all, there must be a free and open admission that these frustrating forces in life exist — that we really are frustrated. We must be ready to admit that we find it hard to face up to these obstacles. Hostility, anger or resentment cannot be controlled if we do not admit that they actually exist. We must be aware of the thing we are trying to conquer. Be ready to admit that you are angry, or that you have hostility. There is no value in trying to fool yourself or in saying, "I am not that kind of person."

Grown people are often like children in this respect. With a flushed face and in an angry tone someone will say, "I am not angry." This is childish. Admit it freely, at least to yourself, for this is the first step you must take.

The second step is to ask yourself the question, "Why do I feel this way?" Often when we begin to analyze our anger, or grief, or resentment, we will find that there is some deeper underlying motive. We are hostile towards a person because we do not like him, or we may be envious of him. We may feel threatened by another person, or may be competing with him, and so our ire is easily aroused. Careful contemplation is always important. Learn to be honest with yourself. For it is always good for us to learn to know ourselves as we really are, not as we would like to be.

The third step is an exercise of the will to overcome the attitude we have developed. Try to change hate to love, resentment into acceptance. Get yourself under contol. You cannot operate efficiently as a person with such strong feelings festering in your heart.

A WORTHWHILE GOAL

The conquest of the self is not easy, but it is important for good emotional health. This is best learned at the time when the will is still supple and the emotional patterns are not too deeply set. It is important that we learn this in our childhood. It is a large part of the training that must be given in the home. For good character traits can best be formed in childhood.

People have often said to me, "I used to have a terrible temper, but I have learned that when I count to ten before I speak, I don't say anything rash." Such a person has not really learned to control his temper; he has only learned to control the symptoms. Self-control means that we master the anger itself.

This is where we must put our Christian faith into practice. The man of the world will speak about adjusting to life's frustration; the Christian speaks about conquering them. For "He that ruleth his spirit is greater than he that taketh a city."

One young lady said that she could learn to control herself by thinking of her deceased father, whom she adored. She would ask, "How would daddy react under such circumstances?" This helped her to win the battle. There is value in this. Even reading the biographies of great men can inspire us.

But the Christian can go further than this. He can look up to His Lord and say, "How would Jesus react under these circumstances?" For He too was tempted like as we are in all things, yet without sin.

But Jesus left not only an example and pattern. He still walks with us and assures us that He will help us to gain the victory. Then self-control is not a grim and dreary battle, but the surrender of self to Him, so that even every thought is brought into captivity to Christ. This is the most powerful means of self-control. Have you tried it?

10. Learning from Our Critics

In an average lifetime everyone must accept a good deal of criticism. We criticize others, and others in turn criticize us. It would seem that some people are in positions where they are more likely to be criticized than in others. In the time of a political election, politicians are bombarded with criticism. Ministers usually get their share of it, and janitors and merchants are not immune. In fact, all of us, no matter what our position is, will get our share of criticism in an average lifetime.

The way we accept criticism is a real test of character. Actually, I do not believe that anyone enjoys criticism. We all look for approval and acceptance and praise, and are disappointed when our superiors or our peers do not approve of the way we do things, or suggest that we could do better.

This world is not a friendly place. One of the first things a young man learns when he pushes out from the protective environment of the home is that he must submit to criticism and opposition. He will not often receive a great deal of commendation and acclaim. This is an atmosphere in which a healthy person can grow, but a weak personality will react unfavorably.

HARSH CRITICS

There are different ways of pointing out the faults of others. One person will do it bluntly and harshly, almost rudely. Another will do it in such a way that it does not humiliate. Great wisdom is required for those who guide the lives of others. There is need for a genuine concern for the feelings of our fellow men.

Paul tells fathers not to provoke their children to wrath, lest they be discouraged. There are parents who often correct their children in an angry tone. They continually tell their children about their faults and seldom praise them. Parents cannot fulfil their duties by nagging and scolding. There must be a gentle concern for the sensitive feelings of a child.

Criticism in the home must be handled with caution. When a husband criticizes his wife's cooking, or her hat, or a wife criticizes her husband's bad habits, it must always be done in a spirit of loving concern for the other. For this can cause great bitterness and many hurt feelings.

OPEN-MINDED ATTITUDE

Still we may learn from our critics, for not one of us has

encyclopedic knowledge. There are always those who know certain things better than we do, and we can learn from them. A famous artist had painted a portrait which he considered to be a masterpiece. But a lowly shoemaker pointed out that the artist had not painted the buckle on the shoe realistically. The artist responded, "What does a shoemaker know about painting?" He forgot however that the shoemaker knew more about shoes than he did.

Face your critic with an open-minded attitude. We all know people who are willing to listen as long as others compliment them or flatter them, but the moment they are criticized are deeply offended and hurt. Anyone who dares to say anything unfavorable about them is considered an enemy.

It is hard to maintain cordial relations with such persons, for no one cares to be a friend of one who listens only to flattery. Such persons view every critical remark as an attack on their own personality, and they feel that they must counter-attack. Such people place themselves above criticism, they carry an air of infallibility. They have cut themselves loose from one of the best means of growth and improvement. They are no longer teachable. They would rather live with their faults than suffer the humiliation of having someone point them out to them. They have closed minds.

Such persons live in a very insecure world, constantly being threatened by attacks from others. No doubt it may hurt our pride to have our faults pointed out to us, but it is better to let the pain work for our improvement than to allow it to work resentment in us.

FACE IT HONESTLY

Face your critics honestly. Try to find out whether the criticism was given with good or evil intention, whether in love or in hate. If your critics are only finding fault in order to cover up their own failings, take it lightly, pass it off as something insignificant.

First of all ask, "Is it true? Do I really have the fault that is mentioned?" We are all a little biased in our opinions of self. There is no real objectivity when we observe ourselves, either in a mirror or in the words and attitudes of others.

Accept criticism as a part of being human. It is only natural that we do not do all things well. It should not be humiliating to receive criticism. Accept it with all humility.

A SENSE OF HUMOR

But also accept it with a sense of humor. Humor helps us to look at ourselves with a sense of detachment, and it helps us to get a good look at our problems. Laugh at yourself at least once a day, for most of us take ourselves too seriously.

Don't place yourself on the defensive. The human inclination is to answer criticism with counter-criticism. This is childish. When a boy tells another boy that he is not a good sport, he is quite sure to get the answer, "Well, don't think you're such a good sport either."

Some never outgrow this attitude. They see all criticism as a personal affront, and they feel that they must strike back to defend themselves. Such people are usually threatened individuals who feel that their own position is rather shaky. When this method is carried to an extreme, you soon begin to feel that all men are against you, that the world does not really understand and appreciate you. Our mental hospitals see their share of such attitudes.

A CONSTRUCTIVE ATTITUDE

Constructive acceptance of criticism will make it serve as a stepping stone rather than a stumbling block. Criticism then becomes part of the highest form of interpersonal relationship, that of helping one another on the road of life.

When we read the Bible earnestly and prayerfully, it will often lay bare our sins and errors. It sometimes condemns our actions, words and attitudes. If we will accept the Lord's correction in humility, this will serve as a means of spiritual growth and help us to gain inner peace.

Paul expresses his view of criticism in his letter to the Corinthians, "But with me, it is a small thing that I should be judged of you, or of man's judgment; But he that judgeth me is the Lord."

11. Too Much of Self

I am sure that we all know a good many self-centered people. A brief conversation with them is soon centered on themselves. They talk about their aches and pains, their accomplishments and their problems. The pronouns "I" and "me" and "mine" flow rather frequently in their speech. Life is viewed in the light of a small and personal world.

Self-centeredness is not only unpleasant to others; it is also dangerous to a person's own mental and emotional health. To be continually thinking and talking about self, to be always wanting more for ourselves, is fertile soil for the growth of a neurotic personality; for the psycho-neurotic turns all things towards himself.

A VERY COMMON ATTITUDE

There is something strange about self-centeredness, even though it is common. Here is a man, a tiny speck in the vast span of time, a little drop in the great ocean of humanity. He is only one of more than 2 billion people who inhabit the world. Yet he seems to feel that the whole world moves only around him, that he stands at the center of all things.

Among the self-centered are the conceited and the selfish. If these people have families, all the members must conform to their every whim. If they have arguments, they are always right. They have a strong desire to be accepted and loved, yet little capacity to love and accept others. The world has a lot of these little people who think in expansive ideas about themselves. In fact, most of us have a little of this in us.

A little self-esteem, a healthy feeling of our own dignity, is normal. But when this is driven to extremes, a person becomes intolerable to live with, and in fact he has a hard time living with himself. For he has the difficult task of living up to the estimate he has of himself.

FOUNDATIONS IN EARLY LIFE

Often self-centered characteristics have their beginnings in childhood. Every child is basically selfish. He must be taught to be unselfish. If children do not learn this in their formative years, they will go through life afflicted with self-centeredness.

Today every boy is taught to work hard to get ahead in this world. He must set his ideals high, for you know, some day he

may be president. The qualities of compassion, kindness and understanding are often sacrificed. Every girl is taught to be glamorous.
Home-making and the rearing of a family take a second place to
the building of a career. If the girl is to marry, her mate must
be able to provide well for her so that she can reach the desired
status.

Now, we would not discourage healthy ambitions and the seeking
of a worthy career. Nor would we discredit those that try to get
ahead in life. There is a natural craving in us for the things that
make life worthwhile. We should be ambitious.

UNHEALTHY AMBITIONS

But we must discourage our tendency to become self-centered
and self-seeking creatures, whose chief concern is to pursue our
own comfort and satisfaction. This is wrong and dangerous. This
leads people to play life for their own advantage. Here lies one
of the great weaknesses of our generation. There is too much of
self. There is danger that we are training children and young
people who are basically selfish, who think too much in terms of
personal gain and too little in terms of personal service. Many
have become so near-sighted that they cannot see the needs of a
bleeding and dying world that lies across the street; they pull back
their skirts and pass by on the other side.

Selfishness leads men to an outlook on life that is too narrow,
a view of life that is too small. It robs men of one of the great joys
of living, that of giving instead of getting. Often, when persons
with problems of an emotional or nervous nature come to see our
psychiatrists, they are sent home with the advice to go out and
do something for others. Many women find a great deal of emotional
help for themselves by volunteering as Grey Ladies and aides in
hospitals, or throwing their influence and interest behind some
worthwhile cause.

Other people have found help by giving active assistance in
mission work, or helping an overburdened teacher, or helping a
handicapped person. Too many of the emotionally disturbed are
bored and hence begin to think of everything in terms of self. It
is important to learn to think in terms of others.

LEARNING UNSELFISHNESS

The real lessons of selflessness are learned at the feet of Jesus.
The Master of souls tells a beautiful story about a young man who
was too self-centered. It is the story of the prodigal. As a young
man he goes to his father with outstretched palm and says, "Father,

give me." It was the immature request of a selfish young man. He wanted only to satisfy his own human desires.

But he is rather a modern figure, for there are many who take the "give-me" attitude towards life. Many are only interested in what they can get out of life. This may be one of the reasons why there is usually a shortage of ministers, missionaries, teachers, nurses and doctors. This is possibly also the reason why there are so many members of the church who are just satisfied to sit in the pew on Sunday to drink in the message of Life, but who cannot be motivated to be of service, or to witness for the Christ.

THE "MAKE-ME" ATTITUDE

Jesus shows that this attitude leads to the far country, away from Father and home. It brings the prodigal finally to the end of the road. He takes inventory of his assets, and he knows that he is spiritually, morally and emotionally bankrupt. He then moves through a cycle that is familiar to many. He comes to himself, he reflects on his past sins and he says, "I will arise and go to my father, and I will say "Father, Make me . . . .""

This second request rises from the sobs of a broken heart. It is the attitude of one who looks away from self, looks to his father and home, and speaks of a surrendered heart and life.

This is the attitude of a mature Christian, who has moved out of the "baby" stage. It is a healthy attitude, one that thinks of life in terms of giving instead of getting.

This is the sure cure for self-centeredness. It worked in Jesus' day. The cure is still at hand for us today.

12. Faultfinding

Jesus knew the value of humor in dealing with people, and He often used it as an effective weapon. There must have been a glint in his eye when He told the story of the man who had a beam in his eye and who was looking for a splinter in the eye of his brother. Such a picture would naturally make the faultfinder look rather ridiculous.

In spite of Jesus' warning, the faultfinders are still with us today. You will find them in every community, there are some in every congregation, in fact, we may all slip into this bad habit at times. Some are more addicted to this tendency than others. It has been observed that when we judge others, and point out their errors, we are actually revealing our own faults. We hate the evils we see in others, but we may at the same time be nurturing these sins within our own hearts.

Censoriousness, or looking for faults in others, is an evil that poisons our own lives and breaks down our relationships with others. It is no wonder that the Bible frequently warns against it. It is an evil that can and must be overcome, if we are to be effective members of the body of Christ. There are several things we should consider in this matter which may help us to learn to accept others a bit more charitably.

GET ALL THE FACTS

Before we criticize others we must make sure that we have all the facts straight. It is extremely unfair to judge others when we do not have sufficient information upon which to base our judgments. People have been criticized for being miserly in their giving, while actually they were secretly lending sacrificial support to an aged mother, or a handicapped brother. Some have been called lazy while actually they were struggling with hidden handicaps.

It is well for us to determine whether there are extenuating circumstances that contribute to obvious behavior patterns. One of the most important requirements for effective pastoral counseling is to remain non-judgmental towards a person, so that we may learn the deeper inner motives that underlie behavior.

In most cases it will be discovered that things are not always what they seem to be on the surface. It is important to know all the facts before we begin to find fault, and often, when all the facts are known we are far more charitable in our judgments.

OUR OWN MOTIVES

Another way to conquer the censorious spirit is to investigate our motives. Why do we find fault with our sister or brother? There are several reasons. The person that has a feeling of his own inferiority will often find fault with someone whom he secretly feels is superior to him. He feels threatened by the other person and so he strikes out with unjust and bitter criticism. This is one of the mental defense mechanisms that is often used.

We may also find fault with others because we envy them. It may be an expression of hostility towards one whom we do not like, or someone who has stepped on our toes. A nurse may find fault with another nurse, in order to build up her own ego. But she forgets that she can never build up herself by tearing another person down.

One of the most common experiences in faultfinding is that we see sins in others which we recognize so well because we also have the same errors in our own life. It eases our consciences a bit when we can point to the stains that other people have on their characters, and helps us to forget our own failings.

We will be able to find in the lives of others what we are looking for. If we look for the worst we will be sure to find it, but if we look for the best we will also be able to find that. When a girl is in love with a young man she will have a hard time seeing any of his faults. But if the mother of the young lady does not approve of her daughter's suitor she will have a hard time finding any good qualities in him. It depends upon our viewpoint.

One Sunday you went to church in a faultfinding mood. The music was not to your liking, the sermon did not strike home with you, you even criticized the dress of a fellow-member, and you were sure that the janitor had made the temperature too hot. You were looking for faults, and you found them. But all the while you had a beam in your eye so that you could not see straight. The faultfinder is a bad fact-finder.

CHRISTIAN CHARITY

Careful examination will reveal that a censorious person is one who has lost his charity toward his brother. He sees the worst in him, instead of the best. He sees this because his love has turned into hostility.

A boy comes home after a bad day at school. Things have not

gone well for him, either in the classroom, or on the playground. When he comes to the table the food is not to his liking. He criticizes his brothers and sisters and he finds fault with everything that meets the eye. He has developed a hostile attitude.

Many people go through life that way. They transfer their hostile feelings towards others. Instead of looking into their own hearts to find the cause of their feelings, they take them out on others. The faultfinder is basically a hostile person, revealing his aggression.

The best way to overcome this is to pause for a moment to ask ourselves why we feel the way we do. A prayerful self-examination will reveal that though there may be splinters in the eyes of our brother, we actually have a large beam of prejudice and hostility in our own eye. We can only help our brother when we first remove the beam from our own eye.

There is much hostility even among members of the same church. But there is a place where we together may bow, at the feet of One who knows the faults of all of us, and there we may pray, "Forgive us our debts, as we forgive our debtors."

13. Inconsistencies

Most of us are acquainted with the story of Dr. Jekyll and Mr. Hyde. It gives an account of a man who was at one time a benefactor of society, and at other times he was a fiend with murderous intent. It portrays an extreme example of dual personality. We may be thankful that the world has seen but few of this extreme type.

But there are strange inconsistencies in many people, in fact none of us is completely consistent in all things. We generally tend to develop a blindness to the contradictions in our own character, while we see clearly those in our relatives and friends.

OUTSTANDING EXAMPLES

It is not hard to find examples of obvious inconsistencies. It may be seen in leading men in the field of business or the professions. Such men may be liberal givers for the community and the Kingdom. They may even be Sunday school teachers, or members of the consistory. But when they are out in the business arena they reveal a different side of their character. They drive a hard bargain and may not be reluctant to ruin the business of a competitor. Their religion requires a love for their fellowmen on Sunday, which may be strangely lacking during the week.

There are others who are staunch defenders of the faith. They may labor hard to preserve the purity of the church. But at the same time they reveal a strange lack of love for those who dare to differ with them.

There have been other leaders in the church, men with ability and zeal for the kingdom, but they are hard to live with at home. They reveal a good Christian spirit in one area of life, but they are devoid of this spirit in another area.

Children and young people may manifest this same dualism of character. Out on the streets among their peers, or in the social setting, they are such good sports, and manifest such a congenial spirit. But when they are at home with their parents and brothers and sisters they can be regular little scoundrels.

COMPARTMENTALIZATION

Why do people develop such inconsistencies in their personality? What has happened in such lives? These people have developed neat, logic-tight compartments in life. They have developed a form of segregation in the pattern of living. This can be the case to such an extent that you can say of some people, "they are like two different persons."

This is one of the methods that is used to resolve certain conflicts in life. Where there are two or more strong conflicting desires or drives, they do not resolve the conflicts, but they merely split up life into various areas. And they circumvent the conflict by compartmentalization. They even begin to feel that the various areas of life can be allowed to exist along side of each other, as unrelated and separate compartments.

EXTREME CASES

We frequently see extreme examples of such contradictions in the people who must be hospitalized. Among them are the so-called psychopathic persons, those who are continually getting themselves into trouble by their behavior. One of the things that characterizes their life is that they do not learn from experience.

These anti-social persons may be very attractive personalities. They are pleasant to talk to, and can often carry on fine spiritual conversations. If we were not aware of their history we might say that they are good Christians. But as soon as they are on their own resources, they again drift into trouble. They move from one deceptive scheme to another.

It would not be correct to say that such segregation causes the severe mental illness described as schizophrenia, or split personality. But such sufferers often live in two or three different unrelated worlds.

Alcoholics frequently fall into this category also. They too may be attractive and capable persons. But they cannot survive the temptation for drink, and so fall into a socially unacceptable pattern of living.

A POSITIVE SUGGESTION

We all have a measure of inconsistency in us. But we may never be satisfied with this. We never quite reach the point that our doctrine and our life agree perfectly, but we surely must strive for this. Our walk and our talk should agree.

Is it not true that we are also in danger of dividing life into neat little compartments, so that all of life is not brought under the sway of mighty convictions?

The person with excessive worries does that. His faith in the providence of a loving Father has never quite reached down to everyday life. The materialist also has split life into logic-tight compartments. So does the sensualist, the seeker after pleasure, and the inconsistent church member.

We need a unifying principle strong enough to bind life into one great whole. This principle must be more than a doctrine, more than a creed, for it can be found only in a Person.

It is found only in the pathway of surrender to the inescapable Christ. For when we place all the conflicting desires and drives of life under one all-embracing desire, we will have united our personality. When we bring every thought into captivity in obedience to the Christ we will have healed the separation between all the areas of life. This brings unity into a heart that is torn asunder by sin.

"Unite my heart to fear Thy Name."

14. Prejudice

Prejudice is an evil that has plagued mankind for many centuries. The Romans and Greeks viewed all other nations, including our fore-fathers, as Barbarians. In the days of Jesus there was a strong racial conflict between the Jews and the Samaritans.

Today there are large barriers of prejudice between the races. This has become a sticky problem in the United States, in South Africa, and even causes concern in England.

I am sure that all of us have a certain amount of it, in spite of the fact that the Christian faith should teach us that the God we serve deals with man "without respect of person."

PERSONAL PREJUDICE

The word "prejudice" finds its root meaning in an act of pre-judging, that is, to form an opinion about someone else in the absence of all the facts. It forms judgments of people for reasons other than what they are as persons.

Prejudice is something that grows in the developing personality. A little child must learn to get along with other children. At first this takes place in the home, but as he grows older this circle of persons, with whom he must relate, becomes larger. In time he will have friends outside of the home, and he must even learn to relate to strangers. This reaches out also to those of different races, religions and languages.

Personal prejudice implies that one has been stunted in his social growth. He has developed to a point where he can get along with his wife, his family, his fellow-workers and his fellow-church members, but he is uncomfortable when he meets someone outside of this circle. He feels ill at ease when he meets a Catholic, a Negro, a Jew, or a Russian. Today our world makes higher demands for social growth than was required in days gone by. Today we must be able to meet the stranger and relate to him. Many are not ready for this and hide back in a shell of prejudicial feelings.

Back of all individual prejudice lies the sin of pride. It is the attitude that we are better than others, and for that reason we are not willing to accept those who are different from us. This is very obvious in the race relationship. Why should we consider a white skin to be superior when only one-fifth of the world is white and four-fifths is of a different hue?

GROUP PREJUDICE

We tend to draw lines of distinction between various groups, and then find it hard to see that there is any good in the group to which we do not belong. Usually, there are no reasonable bases for these feelings; they rest on immature emotions. I can well remember that in the early days of my ministry there were people within the church who were strongly prejudiced against all things that were presented in the English language. They were sure that the Christian faith could be presented and defended far better in the Holland tongue.

It is of a great importance to the cause of Christ that these group prejudices be broken down. The racial discrimination in our land is doing great damage to the missionary voice that comes from America. For a native Nigerian it is hard to understand that we as a church are willing to spend millions of dollars for missionary work in Africa, but we do not want to live on the same street with one of the same race.

CONQUERING PREJUDICE

It is important that we develop the habit of thinking of others as God thinks of them.

In a family there were two little boys who had quite a bit of rivalry between them. When the father came home in the evening he picked up one of them, and the little boy responded with a warm embrace and said, "I love you, daddy." But while he was embracing his father he stuck out his tongue at his little brother.

There are many like that today. Standing before God, they are ready to say, "Our Father, who art in heaven." But their prejudiced heart breathes hostility towards another one of the Father's sons. They may be willing to say with the elder brother, "This, Thy son." But the Father still says, "This, thy brother."

15. Let's Stop Pretending

In time of war a very common term is the word "camouflage." By taking advantage of the laws of visual perception, gun emplacements, transports and even men can be so disguised that to the enemy they appeared as harmless objects.

There is also a lot of mental and emotional camouflage. We often try to conceal what actually goes on within us. We use masks to hide our true identity and to conceal our real selves. We cover up our inner motives and desires so that they will appear acceptable and even praiseworthy.

Pretense is very common in everyday life. It is taken for granted that it is acceptable to hide our inner feelings in words that actually express a lie. I am sure that most of us have said to a person whom we have casually met on the street, "How nice to see you," while actually we were thinking in our hearts, "I wish I could have avoided meeting her." The salesman, the merchant, the person interested in establishing good public relations often use winning words when basically, they are hiding their real feelings.

Naturally, social graces require that we do not say everything that comes into our minds. We need not be rude and boorish in our personal contacts. But there are some real dangers in pretending.

COMMON PRETENSES

If someone asks you about the work that you are doing, most likely your account of your accomplishments will be a bit more glowing than that of your boss or your secretary. We put ourselves in the best possible light.

Many pretend to know more than they really do. If you listen to conversations about satellites, politics, psychology or even religion, you soon notice that fancy terms will often cover up a lot of ignorance about a subject.

Often when ministers are present people will pretend to be far more religious than they actually are. Even among those who never attend church there are those who indicate that they are quite religious, especially when they are trying to sell something. I am inclined to believe that many families pretend to be more religious when a pastor or an elder comes to visit. This is a form of spiritual camouflage.

There are ugly masks that people wear. A man may express insults and caustic criticisms and then tell us that he believes in being honest, candid and sincere. Others like to tell about the latest scandals and evils. They express great indignation and call for reforms, but actually are finding a convenient way to cover up their own evils.

Others parade as humble souls in order to hide their inner pride. Some take on a boastful attitude to hide their feelings of insecurity. The man who "protests too loudly" is often one who has something to hide in his own life.

There are many forms of pretending, but no person can be really happy about it. When we pretend, we cannot relax even for a minute; we must be constantly on guard, because we live in the danger that others will find out what we are really like. We are always threatened, and so must keep up a front. Living with pretenses is dangerous business because it produces unnecessary tensions.

This does not mean that we are always aware of the camouflage that we are using. Our emotions often play strange tricks on us, for few of us dare to reveal our real selves. We do our best to hide our inner natures. It may be well that it is so, for we should not parade our weaknesses before others. Enough of the bad that is in us is evident to others.

But it is most important that we remove our masks when we are alone and when we look in the mirror of our own hearts. Robert Burns, the Scottish poet, suggests that it would be good for us to see ourselves as others see us. This can be a very revealing thing. Others view our lives more objectively than we do ourselves. But, even more important, we should learn to see ourselves as God sees us.

WHY PRETEND?

Just why do people go to such extremes to build up an elaborate front? You and I want to be somebody; we want recognition from the world around us, and some response from those with whom we live and work. Often our desire for recognition leads us to pretenses. We want others to think well of us.

Another reason for hanging on to these camouflages is that we cannot face ourselves as we really are. As we try to impress others, we are also trying to impress ourselves. The tragedy is that we often rest on outward props rather than on inward values. We compensate for our inward inadequacies by seeking outward recognition. This gives the beauty parlors and the makers of cosmetics and hair-restorers a thriving business.

As a rule, an extreme and elaborate form of building pretenses is evident in the neurotic person. Dr. Karen Horney, a noted psychiatrist, notes that the predominant characteristic of a neurotic is the "excessive dependence upon the approval and affection of others."

DROPPING OUR PRETENSES

To overcome the unhappy lot of the pretender requires that we learn to face reality. There are always others that know more than we do, and it is no disgrace to have to say "I don't know," for no one is expected to know all things. We must remember too that we are neither genius nor saint. All of us have fears and weaknesses, emotional highs and lows, and hearts that are stained with sin.

But at the same time we should strive to learn to know the place which God has chosen for us in His plan, the place where we can make our own distinct contribution. And the only way we can make that contribution is to be ourselves. We can never be our best self when we pretend to be more than we really are. We must not be playing a role, we must be living a life.

God has given to each of us certain resources. Never minimize these. Be honest with yourself and develop these resources to the highest possible degree. Let's stop pretending and transform the energies spent in camouflaging our lives into creative Christian living. You will be surprised at the satisfaction this will give.

Jesus had a remarkable way of tearing away the masks of the men and women of his day. He revealed the true nature of the Pharisees, of His disciples, of the rich young ruler and of Martha. The Bible is painfully frank when it records the biographies of the characters of Scripture. It does not omit the dark and smudged sections.

But the real unmasking comes for each of us when we enter into the presence of God, and when in solitude we pray, with David, "Search me, O God, and know my heart; try me and know my thoughts." No pretenses can long remain in the presence of such prayer. And real spiritual growth and maturity can be found only when the masks are removed and we move forward, as those who are "pure in heart."

16. Anger

In the beginning of human history God said to Cain, "Why art thou wroth? and why is thy countenance fallen?" Ever since that time men, women, and children have been subject to this emotion of anger. It is a strong emotion, sometimes an overpowering one. It is one of the most common ones and yet one of the most dangerous. I am sure that all are subject to it at times.

You can see it already in a little baby. If you hold an infant so that his movements are restricted he will cry in anger and struggle to be released. As he grows older he will show this anger in more aggressive ways. The extreme of such rage is seen when the child goes into a temper tantrum. It is also not uncommon for children to strike out at each other, or to pull other's hair.

As people grow older they begin to see that such ways of expressing their wrath are not socially acceptable. They then reveal that they are angry by words, by deeds that hurt the other person, and even by angry glances.

WHAT CAUSES ANGER?

There are differences in people. There are some things that will arouse one person, but will not affect another. In general, the most common cause of anger is frustration, especially if one is frustrated by an act of another person. This means that the other person stands in our way and so we cannot get our own way.

One of the amusing dramas of the highway is to see two angry motorists shouting at each other, honking their horns, or even shaking their fists. It is often a childish reaction which results when the one car has impeded the progress of the other. One is then acting on the same principle as that of the baby held down too tightly in his crib.

When our goals and desires are thwarted, it tends to threaten us as a person. We want something, and circumstances do not allow us to achieve it, and then we are angry. Basically, it touches our self-esteem, it hurts our pride. We feel threatened by the actions of others, and if we could, we would strike back. But in our present society we cannot live like Lamech, so we do not wound by the sword, but by a word or a hostile deed.

RESULTS OF ANGER

It is a common knowledge that when our wrath is aroused our

57

heart begins to beat vigorously, our breath comes faster, and our hands, or even our whole body will begin to tremble. It often causes lack of sleep and appetite. It is not at all unusual to find a person who persists in hostile attitudes developing indigestion. This is one of the dangers of allowing anger to become chronic.

Anger can sometimes undo what has been built up through many years. Friendships can be shattered and shriveled by one unrestrained explosion of anger. The Christian witness can be hopelessly impaired by it. But worst of all is the result it has on the individual himself. For an angry man is a man at war against himself.

It is hard to understand that people will continue to be angry at someone else for a long time, even for years. Each time they see this person the old hostility will be aroused. Sometimes this can begin with trifling events. Neighbors have sometimes feuded for many years about the placing of a line fence.

It robs man of his inner joy and peace of heart and soul. The angry man is never a happy person, for it is always a disturbing and disrupting emotion.

HOW TO CONQUER ANGER

To gain the victory over our tempers requires a lifelong education. It should begin with children. Parents should strive to teach their youngsters not to continue in anger. Naturally, to do this, we must also show this in our own lives.

The temper tantrums of children are not something to make parents unduly alarmed. A little child, when frustrated, will at times say to his mother, "I hate you." Possibly you have done this once or twice when you were younger, you didn't really mean it, it was said in a fit of rage.

When temper tantrums persist into adult life they are real sources of danger. A child may lie on the floor and kick and scream, but when mother starts to throw dishes, or father shakes his fist in his neighbor's face, it is quite a different story. Parents who punish their children in a fit of anger usually live to regret it. For this is the law of retaliation, and it has no place in the Christian life.

"Let not the sun go down upon your wrath" is wise advice. Do not allow it to fester in your heart. When the feelings of anger and indignation arise, face them squarely. It is not good to say, "I am not angry." Rather say to yourself, "Why are you angry?" And when you try to answer that question you will find a strange answer. You will discover that basically you are angry because something threatens your self-esteem, it hurts your pride.

When you so approach your anger you will soon say to yourself, "Wasn't that a silly thing to get worked up about?" To be sure there is such a thing as righteous wrath, or holy anger, but that is quite a different thing from what we see in our lives. Most of our anger is sinful.

Learn to conquer your anger at the feet of Him who, "when he was reviled, reviled not again." He did not have to strike back, because He did not feel that His personality was being threatened. He ruled His own spirit in a magnificent way. Even when His eyes flashed with holy indignation, and He had a whip in His hand, He had complete control of Himself.

"Learn of me, for I am meek and lowly in heart."

17. Developing Self-confidence

In every congregation there are members who say, "If I only had more self-confidence I would be willing to teach a Sunday school class, or lead in public prayer." There are many who lack confidence in their own abilities. Some are unwilling to express their own ideas until someone in whom they have confidence expresses the idea first.

My father used to tell of a congregation in which there was one dominant leader. Whenever a minister preached in that church the people would first see whether this leader was pleased with the sermon before the rest of the people would shake hands with the minister, and tell him they enjoyed the sermon.

Many people are either unable or unwilling to think for themselves. On national issues they must obtain their opinions from a favorite news magazine or commentator. When it comes to religious issues they follow the opinions of editors of religious periodicals, or the expressions of trusted leaders. In congregational meetings, or school society meetings, they wait to hear what certain other individuals have to say, and this molds their decisions and influences their vote.

I am convinced that this lack of confidence is instilled by training and education which leaves little room for independent thought and action. Many are taught to follow the leader, and they do this slavishly.

This brings serious problems when such persons are confronted with choices for which there is no prescription and no leader. They have not learned to think for themselves, hence they flounder on a sea of indecision. A person who lacks trust in himself, in his own opinions and abilities, is never quite at ease, and is not reaching the God-given goals for his life.

I am not thinking here of people with an inferiority complex. Such persons need professional help and guidance, for in them the feeling of inferiority has become a pattern of living. I am thinking of a much larger group of people, who lack the confidence they need to live positively and constructively.

How can we gain greater self-confidence? There is no simple formula that can be given, and there is no easy road to achieve the goal. Dr. J. A. Hadfield, in his book *Psychology and Morals* says, "There are three principles of psychological and moral health; know

60

thyself; accept thyself; be thyself." If we will take these three steps we will be moving toward greater self-confidence.

KNOW THYSELF

We need to take careful inventory of both our assets and our liabilities. This is not a single act but a process of education. We cannot find out what we are really like merely by looking in a mirror. The true knowledge of self requires a deeper searching of our lives, our attitudes, our past experiences, and our goals and ambitions for living. This is a lifelong process.

We are quite prejudiced with regard to ourselves, and the picture of the self is distorted because it is conditioned by all the experiences of childhood and by the society in which we live. Various things have happened which bring on feelings of inferiority and inadequacy. Some of these feelings have no basis in fact at all.

Paul tells us that a man should "not think more highly of himself than he ought to think." Nor should a man think less of himself than he ought to think. The Bible often emphasizes the dignity of man as the image-bearer of God, and as a child of the King. Hence we may not move through life as a cowering individual always afraid of our own shadow, but we are called to move through this world with the free and swinging step of one who knows that this is his Father's world.

ACCEPT THYSELF

A good inventory of self will reveal that we all have certain limitations. There are always areas of life in which we will be inferior to others. As ministers we may develop considerable confidence on the pulpit, or while teaching a Bible class, but we would feel most inadequate at the top of a ladder or trying to repair a stalled automobile. None of us can excel in all things. We must expect that others will excel us in some areas of life. It is important to accept this fact. We are expected to gain a measure of confidence in the sphere of life in which God has placed us, but we need not feel bad when others excel us in other areas of life.

If we can really accept this fact we will not worry about the accomplishments of others. The real feeling of inferiority is that we feel inferior to others, and that we allow this fact to threaten us. In the parable of Jesus the man with one talent was not responsible to accomplish the results expected of the man with five talents. He was required to do his best with what he had.

BE THYSELF

To be yourself means to be your best self, not your lowest self;

to seek to gain the highest level of achievement within your capacities and your place in life. This is required of the child of God. It has often been said that most people reach less than ten per cent of their true potentialities with which they have been endowed.

At best we are all imperfect, and this is a reality we must face honestly. In this way we learn that we cannot trust ourselves completely. We are dependent creatures whose ultimate confidence must be placed in a perfect and all-sufficient God. But He has invested each of us with talents. If we search ourselves diligently we will be surprised by the treasures we find, often buried under years of neglect. We gain confidence as we use these God-given potentialities within us.

The lack of confidence always implies an element of selfishness. We think too much in terms of self, of what others will think of us or say about us. We must move from self-consciousness to self-confidence. The law of the Kingdom is; if you lose yourself sacrificially you will find yourself.

QUALITIES OF CHRISTIAN CHARACTER

Who can discern his errors?
Clear thou me from hidden faults.
Keep back thy servants also from presumptuous sins
Let them not have dominion over me;
Then shall I be upright,
And I shall be clear from great transgressions
Let the words of my mouth
and the meditation of my heart
Be acceptable in thy sight,
O Jehovah,
my rock,
and my redeemer.

— King David, in Psalm 19:12-1

18. A Cheerful Heart Is a Good Medicine

When people sink into the gloom of a depression, and feel the awful despondency which this illness can give, they often think that they will never laugh again. But as they recover they soon begin to smile again, and in due time the merry ring of laughter is heard from their rooms. Laughter is a sign of health. One of the marks of Christian mental health is a good sense of humor.

God gave man the power to weep, but also the gift of mirth. We can catch the emotional response of the gloom of life, but also the humor of life. There were times when people thought that a Christian should not laugh. Crudens, the noted author of the Concordance of the Bible, wrote, "To laugh is to be merry in a sinful manner." That was in 1769.

Unfortunately there are still people today who seem to have that feeling. There are those who think, and even say, "What is there to laugh about today?" With rumors of war, atomic bombs, juvenile delinquency and great apostasy, they feel there is no room for mirth. But the lack of ability to find humor in life is a sign of poor mental health.

My father was a stern prophet of God in the pulpit, but one of the fondest memories I have of him is the ring of his hearty laughter. I can well recall other leaders of our church in days gone by, who would visit our home, and there always was a good deal of enjoyment and mirth.

TRUE HUMOR

But there is much that passes for humor that is irreverent, or cynical, or possibly even suggestive. I like the definition which Macaulay gives us, "Humor is mirth consistent with tender compassion for all that is frail, and with a profound reverence for all that is sublime. If we are to see life as it is, we must see the great and solemn truths which come to us, but we must also see the lighter touches of life. He who has never smiled at the antics of a monkey or of a kitten or of a puppy has lost touch with certain basic realities of life."

WHAT IS FUNNY?

A sense of humor is a very interesting psychological study. There are certain things that seem funny to one person, but not to another. Some people find "Yankee-Dutch" readings very amusing;

personally I find them rather dull. It would be interesting to discover why this is so. Here each person has a right to his own feelings. But we must see to it that our humor is clean and free from any trace of irreverence. It should not be an expression of malice. I see nothing funny in jokes that involve psychotic patients, nor do I like humor which concerns excessive drinking. These areas of life are so tinged with tragedy that humorous stories about them are always off-color.

On the other hand we must beware lest we take ourselves so seriously that we feel offended when people laugh at us. There are people that can laugh heartily when the joke is at the expense of others, but they cannot take a joke in which they are involved. Such people are too easily threatened. They are like a child who makes a mistake and then, instead of laughing at his mistake, begins to cry. They feel that they have failed, and their ego is threatened. Such people have feelings of insecurity.

God gave us humor, and we must use it as an outlet for our emotions. How often the irritations of life can be resolved in moments of cheer and pleasantry. Frequently tensions in a consistory meeting or a synodical gathering are broken when there is a burst of laughter. Tensions in a home can also be broken in the same way. Often the tensions in our own hearts can be resolved, if we could sit down and laugh at ourselves a bit more.

CHRISTIAN HUMOR

Surely, humor characterized the ministry of Jesus. I can imagine that His audience broke into laughter when He told about the man swallowing a camel, or when He pictured the man with a beam sticking out of his eye while he was trying to pluck a little speck out of his neighbor's eye. I would find it impossible to think of Jesus as being truly human, if we would exclude laughter from His life. He was the man of sorrows, but there was also a healthy laughter that bubbled up from the deep sense of joy in His soul.

And, after all, who has more right to humor than the Christian? The man of the world may laugh, but it is a hollow laughter, shallow and empty. The Christian, however, has a deep fountain of joy, which still runs clear and full when the cisterns of this world have run dry. He has a humor which only his faith made possible.

We all long for a victorious faith. One of the ingredients of that perspective of life is the ability to smile, even when the going is a bit rough. Our Lord said in one of the darkest moments of His life, "Be of *good cheer,* I have overcome the world." He had the sorrows of the world on His heart, but He had the joy of heaven in His soul.

This is also what Solomon had in mind when he tells us that "A *cheerful* heart is a good medicine" (Proverbs 17:22). For some people I know, it is the best medicine. For humor is one of the important allies of faith.

19. Can You See Straight?

If we would visit an African jungle we would notice that the natives see and hear things that we cannot perceive. They easily detect a slight stir in the underbrush. Their ears are tuned to hear the padded footfalls of the lion, and they have an amazing ability to read the tracks of game animals.

A mechanic will hear telltale noises in your car that you may not have noticed. A physican will diagnose illnesses from a set of symptoms that the average layman scarcely observes. A mother sees things in her child and detects what is wrong from the way he cries, things that a stranger would not detect.

This shows that we see what we are prepared to see or have been trained to see. A rather familiar story is told about four men who stood on the brink of the Grand Canyon of the Colorado at sunset. The geologist busied his mind with the light as it reflected itself on the various strata of rock. The poet thought of life as pictured by the dying day. The painter watched the various hues of red and yellow and purple. The real estate promoter thought of building a restaurant, with large picture windows and good prices for food in such a setting.

SELECTIVE PERCEPTION

We all tend to see things in the light of our own interests, our training and our perspective on life. This is called selective perception. This is true for all of us. None of us is really objective in the way we look at life and its problems. The way we see others, our interpretation of the facts of life, depends upon our own emotional background and our sense of values.

INK-BLOT TESTS

A European psychiatrist, Hermann Rorschach, found in this fact a tool that can be used to test what we tend to see, and possibly, why we see things the way we do. He took some large cards and put ink-blots on them. These strange figures do not actually represent any particular object, but they can be interpreted by one person as one thing and by other persons as another thing.

This Rorschach test is used by psychologists as an instrument to discover what a person sees. One person may see in the black figures a bird with wings, another may see a face with large ears, a third may see the map of an island. Experts have found out that what one sees in these ink-blots is an index of emotional adjustment to life. Naturally, no test is infallible, but it is a great help to determine the pattern of a personality.

BIASED VISION

We often see what we are prepared to see, or what in the depths of our hearts, we really want to see. The mother who is very fond of her son cannot understand how her son could be interested in a certain girl. The boy, who is very much in love with the girl, can see no fault in her. Possibly, due to their emotional involvements, neither the mother nor the son is seeing straight.

We who live north of the Mason-Dixon line cannot understand the attitude of the Southerners to the race question. The man from the south cannot understand our attitude. Both look at the problem from a different emotional and historical background. It is a question which of the two is seeing straight.

In a labor dispute, the laboring man tends to see the employer as a man who is trying to exploit labor. Management looks at the dispute from the standpoint of industry. It is often hard to determine which of the two sees it correctly.

A PROPER APPROACH

It is well for us to admit that none of us sees all sides of a given object. We tend to see things as they appear to us from our own little corner. If we carry this one-sided view too far, we are in for trouble. It is dangerous to a person's mental health, it constitutes a social problem for it leads to bias and prejudice and intolerance.

How many times have we not pondered the remark made by a friend and asked, "Just what did she mean by that remark?" If we are biased in our vision, we are bound to think the worst.

Learn to see that others may be seeing just as straight as do we. There is the danger that people develop the idea, that there are only two sides to an issue, the one we hold to, and the wrong one. Parents sometimes do this with their children, forgetting that sometimes children also see things straight.

We must ask ourselves, "Do I really see straight?"

Oh yes, there is a standard of values by which we live. There is an authority before which all men must bow. This is true when we come and say, "It is written." For when God speaks, He sees all things aright. For He has an all-seeing eye, an eye that looks beyond the visible, and He is not afflicted with emotional bias.

20. Relaxation

Dr. Cabot described life as a wheel with four spokes. These spokes are work, worship, love and play. Whenever we allow any of these spokes to become too long or too short, the wheel will be out of balance and we will tend to wobble through life.

All work and no play tips the scales of life in the wrong way. We all need times of relaxation and refreshment, when we get away from our regular work and the ordinary routine of living.

LEISURE TIME

Someone has figured out that there are 8760 hours per year. If we work 40 hours per week and have two weeks of vacation, allow 8 hours per day for sleep and 6 hours for eating, dressing, driving to and from work, we still have 1930 hours for leisure time. As Christians we would deduct another 728 hours for Sundays, which by Scriptural mandate are not our own. That still leaves us 1200 hours per year in which we can choose what we desire to do.

Are we making the best use of these leisure hours? Do we use them as time to refresh ourselves so that we may be the better able to do our work, and also the Lord's work?

RELAXATION IS NEEDED

Recreation and a change of pace are to the mind and emotions what food and fresh air are to the body. It is needful to allow the tightly strung nerves to release the tension that is inevitable in daily toil. You can find many ways of doing this. There are things that can be very relaxing to one person that tend to raise the pressure in others.

Some people enjoy travel, and find it relaxing to watch the changing scenery pass by. Others find it in a home workshop or darkroom. Again others develop more artistic hobbies. Some find it in fishing on a quiet lake or in a rushing stream.

The important thing is that we really relax when we find our chosen vacation or hobby. This is where many fall short. There are those who choose the game of golf. But as they become more involved in the game they begin to be so concerned about their scores that they do not find release from tension but rather build it up. There are women who sew for a hobby, and so it becomes almost an obsession for them; they cannot rest till the garment is completed. It makes them more tense.

Often travelers will have as their goal to cover many miles. They are irritable at other travelers on the road, they worry about night accommodations, and they come home far more tired and tense than when they started.

RELAXATION IS AN ATTITUDE

Actually, relaxation is not to be found in some distant spot in the mountains, or in a tent on a quiet lake away from the crowd. It is something you must develop in the inner recesses of your own life. Some people are tense at a backyard barbecue, while others are relaxed in their daily work. It all depends upon your attitude toward yourself, and toward life with its problems.

Many people have never really learned to enjoy life. To do so you must cultivate a sincere desire to live fully and completely. Set out to achieve worthy objectives, and when you have found them, be sure to enjoy them. Take a little time each day to think of the pleasant and enjoyable things we have received through the grace of God.

We must take life seriously, but we need not take ourselves so seriously. There are times when we should also laugh at ourselves. One of our older pastors gave us some sage advice, when he spoke to us at the Seminary. He told us, "When I catch myself hurrying around and getting all excited about the fact that I have more work than I can do, I sit down at my desk, put my feet on the desk, light my pipe, and I say to myself, 'Now, why am I hurrying so? The good Lord never intended that I should live like this.' "

A BLESSED GIFT

The church today badly needs more cheerful Christians. There is need of more relaxed workers. There should be more men and women who have learned to work to their full capacities because they have also learned the art of relaxation.

To be really relaxed we must know that it is well with our soul. We cannot be relaxed when we are oppressed with a burden of guilt, with concerns both for this life and that which is to come. For release from tensions comes not from the outside but from within.

The person who can relax is one who has learned to take a healthy attitude toward life. This is a gift that is given to those who have given heed to the Savior who still says, "I will give you rest."

21. The Cost of Pride

Do you realize that there is no quality in us which can prove as costly as pride? Pride keeps us from admitting that we are wrong, and it costs us a greater sense of guilt. It is a way in which we try to hide from others the weaknesses we possess, and it often makes us live a lie.

There is possibly no more common reason for lovers' quarrels than pride. It causes bickering and strife in home and family life, because people are too proud to give in. The proud person is always feeling offended because he is not receiving the attention he feels he should have. Pride is unyielding, always demanding, and never tender or considerate. Those who do not overcome this evil tendency pay for it in bitter experiences.

And yet, there is more of pride in most of us than we are aware of.

WHAT IS PRIDE?

There is a distinction between pride and self-esteem. These are two different qualities. A man may say, "I'm proud of my family." These feelings of self-esteem may be well founded. There are families of which a father or mother may well be proud. Actually they could just as well say, "I'm fond of my family." Respect and admiration are good qualities.

But pride means conceit. It means that a man sets himself above his fellows and feels superior to them. It inflates his ego when he can look down upon others. He gives himself a feeling of importance by boasting, swaggering, or by some form of display and show. The modern tendency is toward the affirmation of the ego, the exaltation of self, and toward riding roughshod over others in order to satisfy self-centered feeling.

But usually the proud man thinks himself to be better than he is, and when he is criticized he feels hurt. He thinks that others are jealous of his success, or that they bear a grudge against him. Pride is an attempt to create an impression that we are something we actually are not.

A man of great learning and wisdom does not need to show off. It is the man of little knowledge who must make a display. He does this to impress others, and possibly also to impress himself, for basically, the proud man has a deep feeling of inner insecurity.

This is a costly habit. It is not easy to develop a vocabulary of big words. Besides, the intellectual snob is always in danger of being exposed, and he must always keep his defenses up. Such intellectual pride makes it hard for a person to learn, it places a film over his eyes so that he cannot really enjoy life. A proud man can never feel quite at ease, and he is seldom a happy person.

PRIDE AND HUMILITY

There is perhaps no lesson that Jesus emphasized for his disciples as much as the lesson of humility and the danger of pride. The Lord was a humble teacher, and there was little room for the proud in his company. He taught in simple parables and in homely examples drawn from the sheep and the goats, the grass of the field, and the mother sewing patches on a worn-out coat. In the Kingdom of God there is no room for the proud.

But there is more of pride in most of us than we are willing to admit. You can witness this in the fact that even those in the lowliest positions of life are often most easily hurt. They will say, "Don't you think I have any pride?"

In many of the problems of human relationships, pride plays an important role. Many marriages are needlessly broken because one or both of the parties concerned refuse to give in. Many quarrels in a congregation could have been easily solved if there had been more humility shown. This is part of the high cost of pride.

Our Lord placed a little child in the midst of his disciples as an example to show that the least is the greatest. He taught that humility is the great mark for entrance into the Kingdom. He made clear that there is no room for the proud in the Father's house. This is ultimately the highest cost of pride.

22. The Cost of Friendship

One of the most beautiful descriptions of friendship in all literature is the Bible's own account of the friendship of David and Jonathan. The story is classical. These two young men might well have been rivals, the shepherd and the prince, but their souls were knit together in a beautiful relationship.

When Jonathan was killed in the battle of Mount Gilboa, David uttered the moving words: "O Jonathan, thou wast slain in thy high places. I am distressed for thee, my brother Jonathan. . . .thy love to me was wonderful, passing the love of women. How are the mighty fallen!"

This is a tribute to friendship by one who had a true friend, and lost him. It also reveals that there is a price that we must pay to have a friend and to be one. This is the basic ingredient of this close human relationship. To have a friend we must be willing to pay the cost of being a friend.

WE NEED FRIENDS

I often meet people who complain, "I haven't a friend in the world." This feeling of complete aloneness is usually an expression of inner insecurity. It is the language of despair. Few people are so sure of themselves and of their own resources that they feel they can cope with life all alone. We need others to stand by our side to help us, to give us support, and to be our companions in time of need.

But a deeper need for friendship is a psychic one, one that reaches into our inner emotional life. We all have a need to have a feeling of personal worth. Convince a man that he is worthless, or useless, and you will deprive him of much of his will to live. This is one of the reasons why a depressed person feels so desperate; he has lost his sense of personal worth, and feels unworthy and hopeless.

But a friend is one who thinks well of us, he considers us to be worthy of his esteem and companionship. He is willing to give of himself to us. And even more, a true friend is one who makes us think well of ourselves. This upholds the dignity of the individual personality. Basic to our lives is not only the need to love, but also the need to be loved.

ESTABLISHING FRIENDSHIPS

But some find it hard to establish friendships or to keep friends. These are usually people who cannot readily give of themselves, or they are very easily hurt by what others say or do. They want friends, but they are not ready to pay the price.

Many times people will say, "Our church is such an unfriendly church." Young people will complain about the select groups in their school which make it hard to make friends. There is some truth to these remarks. It is a shame that in some churches a stranger can enter for worship and no one will even speak to him. It is also true that some of our high schools have some well established cliques.

But the person who complains about others being unfriendly is usually personally guilty of the same. They are the ones who keep others a bit at a distance and avoid going out of their way to be friendly. They often do not dare to share in close inter-personal relationships. Many of them, even from childhood, have found it hard to establish and to keep friendships.

It is important to cultivate the art of friendship. Try to find others who have similar hobbies and interests, and share these with them. Join in with the social activities of the church, or the mothers' club in the school, for many find lasting friends there. It is also a good place to find your friends, for they will be Christian friends.

PAYING THE PRICE

But, above all, be willing to pay the price of being a friend, one who remains loyal in spite of the cost. For there are too many fair-weather friends. There are many who are willing to be friends as long as some benefit is to be gained, but they turn aside when it requires more giving than receiving.

Albrecht Durer, a renowned painter, had a true friend. When they were young men, both interested in art, it was decided that Durer would paint while his friend would work to support him. It took many years for the artist to make a name for himself, and by that time his friend's hands were calloused and hardened by toil. To express his thanks to his friend, Durer painted a picture of these hands, and it became his most famous work of art. It was a tribute to a friend who was willing to pay the cost of friendship.

Do you want an example of beautiful and whole-hearted friendship? You can hear it in the words of Jesus, "Greater love hath no man than this, that a man lay down his life for his friends. Ye are my friends, if ye do the things that I command you."

23. Inlet and Outlet

A favorite illustration, often used by ministers, concerns the two bodies of water found in Palestine. The Lake of Galilee is beautiful, fresh and blue, because it is fed by water from the mountain springs; and because it has the Jordan River as its outlet. Far to the south is the Dead Sea; it has an inlet but no outlet. It has become a stinking pool of stagnant water.

The mental life also needs both an inlet and an outlet. If a person is to remain healthy and fresh in his thinking he may not be static, but he must be alert to outside impressions and be ready to express these again in creative ways. In this way the mental powers of man become a channel through which flows an endless stream of thought.

CLOSED MINDS

Some people are opposed to all change, they dislike new ideas. In fact, all of us are a bit resistive to ideas that challenge some of the concepts we have long held. It is sometimes rather disquieting to be called upon to change some thought which we had long held to be true and enduring. We all like the security of a closed system of ideas. It does not require much mental effort to resist change.

The symbol of a closed mind is cocksureness. It resists fresh discoveries and eyes with suspicion anything that is different from the pattern which we have accepted. A person with a static mind is like a rather aged Indian who sits in the door of his hogan and looks with a contemptuous eye at the shining train that rumbles by. This to him is the symbol of modern life, but he is content with his own style of living, and that of his forefathers. He is not interested in the onward progress of civilization.

There are many people who have little inlet to their mental life. They have lost their sense of curiosity, and feel that they know almost everything that is important for them to learn. For them life has lost much of its stimulus, for their education is completed, and the books have been put away.

UNSTABLE MINDS

On the other hand there are many who are impulsive in their mental life. They are always shifting from one opinion and conclusion to another. When a new idea comes along they are ready to take it, but when the next day a contrary idea strikes their fancy, they are ready to accept this also. We say of such that they have no mind of their own.

Such discursive thinking leads to instability, and even to unreliability. You never quite know which way the current will be flowing at a given time. They are ruled more by emotion than by logic, they are swayed by the promptings of the moment, with little regard for the past or for the future. When this spirit grips people in their relationship with religious teachings, they are ready to shift from one church to another and from one sect to the next.

When the sluice gates of the mind swing open so widely and so easily, there is often confusion and a deep sense of insecurity. Consistency is a jewel, much to be desired in the area of our inner selves.

A CREATIVE OUTLET

A constructive mind thinks clearly and expresses itself freely. It is neither granite nor water. It is ready to revise itself, to grow; and yet it guards itself against disconnected enthusiasm. It does not close its circuit to that which is new, and it still clings to that which is old.

To find such balance is not easy. It requires concentrated effort, for it is an undeniable fact that self-expression will also require a certain amount of open-mindedness. If the mind is viewed as a channel, it must take in a fresh stream of ideas and impressions if it is to pass them on again to others. If you do not replenish the store of thoughts, you cannot continue to give expression to them.

REPLENISHING THE MIND

A minister can hardly be expected to make two sermons a week unless he is given the opportunity to replenish his store of knowledge through reading and study. If any of us are to have intelligent conversation, we must also find a source of ideas and material for conversation. This is also the real value of society life in our congregations, especially those classes that require that the members take an active part, and that they are not just expected to sit by in the bleachers while the leader or minister performs for them.

Man must have his inlets and his outlets. What he has appropriated into his mental life will seek for expression. So, to be interesting we will have to widen the sphere of our interests.

Our conversation will often reveal what we have been putting into the stream of our mental life. If we sit back and listen to people talk we begin to wonder sometimes about the furnishings of the mind.

There is a danger that many take in only that which they see on the TV screen, or read in a magazine or daily paper. There are many people who never read a good book.

Above all, furnish the chambers of the mind with thoughts of God and longings for eternity. For then the outlet of our life will also be one in which God has the central place. Fill your mind with the things that are true and honorable, just and lovely, and of good report, for then the "God of peace will be with you."

24. The Art of Forgetting

For good mental health, it is important to live in the present. We cannot afford to take on more than one day at a time, for we must concern ourselves with the opportunities of the moment. Yesterday can be our greatest foe, and there are many who are victims of their own past.

Memory is one of the most priceless gifts of a bountiful Creator. It enriches our lives in a most wonderful way, for by it we live not only in the present, but also in the past. As we move through life, the vast storehouse of memories increases, and we can feast on these rich and varied furnishings that adorn the mind.

But, unfortunately, not all memories are happy ones. There are some that should be blotted out from consciousness, for they haunt us and make life miserable. There are many people who suffer from an overdose of such unpleasant recollections, and it robs them of a sense of inner satisfaction.

PASSIVE FORGETTING

There are many thoughts that slip from our mind unnoticed. Unimportant events and thoughts that do not make a deep impression upon us are soon forgotten, and it is relatively impossible to recall them. It would seem that the mind can retain only just so much, and the trivial things soon drop out in order to make room for more important things. This is passive forgetting. At times this can be very annoying, for instance, when we forget a name which we should have remembered.

In many ways we cannot leave the past behind. The past stays with us in the habits we have formed. It haunts us in the consciousness of guilt that we experience, and in the fact that we have a tendency to repeat the sins of yesterday. Our past experiences are in our blood, our brains and in the expressions we wear on our faces. Our emotional structure is, to a large extent, made up of experiences of the past.

ACTIVE FORGETTING

It is for this reason that we speak about the art of learning to forget. There are thoughts that we must consciously try to forget. These are often the ones that have a strong and disturbing feeling attached to them. Psychologists tell us that we never quite reach the point where such concepts are completely and permanently blotted out of our minds. Most of them can again be recalled, and will at times arise to distress us.

Our memories of the past are usually determined by our present attitudes. Tell me what things you remember best, and I will tell you what kind of person you are. Whether you are coarse or cultured, a man of lofty thoughts or sordid ones, whether you are optimistic or morbid, this will be revealed by the things you call to mind.

The humorist has a mind that is stored with jokes and anecdotes. The philosopher can readily call to mind the systems of reasoning of the world's great thinkers. The cheerful man remembers the joys and happy experiences. The person who is easily offended will vividly remember the past hurts inflicted upon him. Your memory will reveal your temperament and character.

FORGETTING PAST WRONGS

Most of us have a hard time forgetting the fact that someone has hurt us, either by word or deed. There are those who will look down upon an entire race or an entire group of people, because of what one member of that group has done to them.

If someone has deceived you, or cheated you, or done some great wrong to you, learn to forget it. If you do not blot it from your mind, it will most likely turn to hate and bitterness. In that way you will be hurting yourself even more than the other person has hurt you.

A wife of an unfaithful husband said, "I will forgive him, but I will never forget what he has done." The resulting disharmony in that home showed that she had neither forgotten, nor forgiven.

There are others who carry with them throughout all the journey of life the things that have happened to them. Some mourn the loss of a dear one for many years; they may even carry that sorrow with them to the grave. Others will tell repeatedly of some misfortune that has come to them perhaps even twenty or thirty years ago.

Such useless brooding over the losses of life tends to depress a person's outlook on life and to retard both emotional and spiritual growth.

FORGETTING PAST SUCCESSES

There are those who are forever boasting about past successes, either in the material or spiritual world. But their present accomplishments do not match the past successes. They should learn to forget their past successes and to live in the present and for the future, for there are ever new heights to climb.

But you cannot just say to your mind, "Now you must forget." Memory does not work by a sheer act of the will, for in the hours of the night the same thoughts will come fleeting before you. You can no more remove those thoughts from your mind by a mere act of will than you can wipe away the melody of a song that comes into your consciousness.

But you can forget by filling your mind with other thoughts, for then one memory will crowd out another. You can remove the ugly memory by placing a lofty thought in its place. Lay aside the past hurt and insult, the past feeling of hostility, and put in the place of it the feeling of love and sympathetic concern for those who have hurt you. This is learning to forget by displacement.

You can learn to forget about past failures only by thinking of past or present successes. Paul knew this secret; he tells us to forget about the past and "press on towards the goal unto the prize of the high calling of God in Christ Jesus."

FORGETTING PAST SINS

You can blot out the feelings of past sins only when you remember that the Bible still says "He will forgive your transgressions and remember them no more." To truly forget, you must feel this marvelous forgiving love and then also learn to forgive yourself.

When we reach the end of the day, we must take careful inventory of it. We must consider its strength and its weakness, its joys and its sorrows, its blessings and its sins. As we confess our sins, we must lay the day with all its experiences at the feet of God, leaving them with "Him who blots the record, who graciously forgives, then forgets."

Learn, then, to leave the past behind and face the future, building upon the experiences of the past.

25. The Chambers of Imagery

In one of the powerful visions of Ezekiel (Chapter 8) there is the story of the prophet being led by the Spirit and brought to the inner court of the temple in Jerusalem. He is told to dig into the wall. As he does so, he comes to a small door that leads to a dark cavern underneath the temple. Entering that cavern, he sees all manner of creeping things — idols and all kinds of abominations pictured on the walls.

In the cave he sees the elders of Israel, with censers in their hands, worshiping these filthy images portrayed on the walls. Upstairs the worship of God is conducted as usual, but below they worship the idols of the heathen nations.

The angel who accompanies Ezekiel says to the prophet, "Hast thou seen what the ancients of Israel do in the dark, every man in the chambers of his imagery?"

SECRET CHAMBERS

This is a picture of man. There is within each of us the realm of the inner man, the secret chambers of the heart, the chambers of imagery. This inner chamber is the real world of a man, the world of the soul, the mind, the inner self. It lies enshrined in mystic seclusion within the mystery of the personality. It is the most important part of man; yet it lies hidden within.

The chamber of imagery enriches man far above all the other creatures. Here lie the powers of the mind, the feelings, the will, the power to choose, and the power to reason and plan.

But, sad to say, sin has also entered into this inner chamber. Sin always begins within us. The sinful act grows out of a sinful thought and a sinful desire. Before we tell a lie, we have conceived a lie within us.

And there is also a world of sin that remains concealed there. Often there are hidden sins, sins of the thoughts, sins of the imagination, sins of desire. They may never come to expression in an overt act, but they are there.

THE INNER SELF

You are what you are in the depth of your soul. You may wear the garments of the priest, but still be an idolator. You may bring your sacrifices into the temple, but there may still be idols in your imagination.

It is important to look into these inner chambers. The things that furnish these chambers will have a profound effect on your life. They can also undermine your mental and spiritual health. The hidden sin that has never been confessed may one day rise up to haunt you. The inner resentments that lie bottled up there may break out in either physical or emotional disturbances. Hidden faults can rob you of peace of heart and the joys of Christian confidence.

It may not be necessary to bring these inner faults out into the open before men, but it is most important that they be brought to our own consciousness, and that they be freely confessed before God. There are those whom I have known who found no real joy of salvation until they brought these evils out of the chambers of imagery and into the pure light of the presence of God.

THE GOSPEL WITHIN

But the beauty of the gospel message is that God's work also takes place in the inner man. The Spirit of God carries on his work from the inner citadel of man and then carries on his work until He has brought man, with all the qualities of body and soul and mind, into captivity to the Christ.

To conquer self, to bring our lives into conformity with his will, we must strive to conquer our thoughts and our desires. This does not happen all at once, but gradually they must be brought under his loving dominion. This is an important part of the long process of conquering self.

Learn to live so that, as we walk in the chambers of imagery, we will meet Jesus there. But He will only be found there when we have furnished it with the things that are true and lovely and of good report.

26. When We Stand Alone

There are millions of people in this world. Frequent references are made to the population explosion and the over-population of many countries of the world. It is an undeniable fact that in some countries there are more people than the country can feed, and it gives a person a feeling that he is not very important as an individual.

There is the danger that the individual is lost in the throng. But there also is an inescapable aloneness in life. Each of us is alone in many of life's relationships. Each person has certain qualities that he has acquired through heredity and environment that make him different from any other person.

PERSONAL RESPONSIBILITY

No one can live your life for you. There are certain questions that only you can answer; there are responsibilities that only you can meet, there are decisions and choices that no one else can make for you. No one can believe for you, for each person must believe for himself. No one can really do your work for you; only you can do it.

Each person suffers alone. Friends or relatives may give support, doctors can give alleviation, but pain is intensely personal, and often a very lonely experience. Death, too, is an individual experience—one that we face alone.

The times when we stand alone put us to a real test. Many people today are afraid to be alone. To overcome the feeling of being alone, people surround themselves with the sound of a radio or a TV set. Young people frequently use the statement, "Everyone is doing it; do you think I want to be the only one that is different?" Men who travel away from home a good deal will consider the fact that they are alone a good deal of the time as an excuse for drinking and other escapades.

Sometimes we become conscious of the aloneness of life. It can be an overwhelming thought. Elijah felt this when he said, "I only am left." He felt this especially in a time of despondency, when he had a feeling of having failed.

If you are the only Christian in an office, or in your department of a factory, you face the necessity of standing alone. Often, if we falter in our loyalty to our convictions and our duties the opportunity may be lost.

A nurse may be alone with a dying patient; you may be the only one who can minister to a person in an accident. But in a sense this is true of every opportunity that comes our way. We all face times when we can witness, if we have the strength to stand alone.

ARE YOU STRONG ENOUGH?

But how well do we stand up when we are alone? It requires a basic inner security to be willing to be counted among the minority. An insecure person soon becomes overwhelmed by the thought of aloneness. There is always strength in numbers, but there is an inner satisfaction also in being alone.

God never lays responsibilities upon us that we are not able to face. He never sends temptations that we are not able to bear. When we become overwhelmed by our tasks, it usually implies that we are trying to carry more than we should.

There is danger that the man who must stand alone becomes a bit bitter over against others. He feels that others should stand with him, and when they don't he displays bitterness. This kind of resentment indicates that he is not really ready to stand alone.

God does not expect us to take on the responsibilities of others. He expects us to carry our own load, and then to leave the rest to him.

Alone, yet in God's sight we are not alone. He has also counted the seven thousand others who have wept in silence over the sins of Israel. He still knows each one of his sheep by name.

27. Patience—A Dynamic Virtue

Just how patient are we? Can we wait for things to happen in their own good time, or are we so eager for them to happen that we try to hurry them? Impatience is often our greatest enemy, for it makes us so anxious that we spoil the very thing we are seeking to achieve.

The Greek origin of the word "patience" suggests two ideas: forbearance and endurance. It can mean either a willingness to wait or continuance in our endeavor to achieve. Both of these elements should be present in our lives.

LEARNING PATIENCE

A person is not born with patience, it is something he must learn. A baby is one of the most impatient creatures. It is a mark of immaturity when a person cannot wait for the greater goals of life and must be satisfied with lesser ones. As a rule, a child would rather have a dime now than wait for a five dollar bill next Friday.

Patience is not a virtue to be practiced only by the sick and those in prison. There are few qualities of the soul that are more important for inner peace of heart, for in everything in life we must learn to practice patience.

All worth-while accomplishments require a certain amount of time. When you plant a seed in the ground you must wait for the sun and the rain and the nourishment of the soil to do their work. Any attempt to hurry up the process will retard the growth or cause it to be of poor quality. You cannot change the rhythm of life, nor can you force things beyond measure without doing some damage.

God usually works in the realm of nature with calm leisureliness. He has no need to hurry, for He is not limited by time. Jesus, in his earthly ministry, revealed this same method of working. I am sure that the patience of Jairus was tried severely when Jesus was journeying to his home to heal his sick daughter. Jesus even stopped along the way to help others. But he says to Jairus, "Fear not, only believe."

PATIENCE TESTED

There are many things that test our patience. A long period of illness and convalescence can be very trying. It is often for this reason that people become irritable and bored, for time moves so slowly when we are impatient. The fifteen minutes that an impatient husband must spend waiting for his wife on a pre-arranged corner often can seem like an hour.

There are also many little frustrations that try us. We can fly off the handle so easily when we are provoked, especially if the provocation touches us where it hurts most. There are vexations in the home, or at work, or even while driving down the highway, that can cause us to lose our tempers. A tin can will not open, a nail bends under the blows of our hammer, or a golf ball goes into the rough instead of on the green, and our patience is strained.

Often we blame the objects or persons that frustrate us, but the real difficulty lies within ourselves. We must learn to conquer our own natures if we are to learn the art of patience. This is important, for it is the great remedy against becoming panicky.

Men use better judgment when they are calm, but when impatient their reason will be impaired. Here lies also one of the great values of the discipline of self-control.

But patience is not a passive virtue; it is a dynamic one. Too often we picture patience as sitting with folded hands, waiting for the inevitable to happen. "Let us run with patience" says the writer of the Book of Hebrews. "In your patience ye shall win your souls" has been translated by Dr. Moffatt, "In your perseverance ye shall win your souls."

PATIENCE EXERCISED

Anyone who has learned a language knows that to do so requires patience, but also activity. Everyone who plays an instrument knows well how much work and patience are required.

It is the patient struggle that helps us win in the battles of life. And when we are tempted to be impatient it is well to look to our Lord, who is still the Author and Finisher of our faith. He reveals great patience in all that He did, and in all his dealings with us.

A person who believes that there is nothing beyond this world cannot be patient, for he has so little time to satisfy his desires and wants. The more materialistic people are, the more they will be in a hurry. Is this possibly why we have become so tense and agitated in our generation?

But the Christian can move on through this world with confidence and serenity, for he sees that the accomplishments of this life are but stepping-stones to eternity. Like the mountain-climber, he patiently chooses his course and carefully takes each step, while he stedfastly keeps his eye fixed toward the mountain-top. And then, each step leads on to the heights.

LIVING WITH OUR EMOTIONS

Oh that I knew where I might find him!
That I might come even to his seat!

Behold I go forward,
but he is not there;
And backwards,
but I cannot perceive him.
On the left hand when he doth work,
but I cannot behold him;
He hideth himself on the right hand,
that I cannot see him.

But he knoweth the way that I take;
When he hath tried me,
I shall come forth as gold.

— Job, in Chapter 23

28. That Tired Feeling

The commercials on radio and television have loudly presented various remedies for that tired feeling. There is one drug that is supposed to help you if you happen to have "tired blood." Evidently, there is a good market for such nostrums, for there are many who suffer from fatigue.

We all talk about being tired at times. Whether this be a hardworking laborer, a mother in a home, a secretary at her desk, or the man who has "banker's hours," all frequently complain of fatigue. Some who are physically or emotionally ill will say that they are always tired. The lazy man will say that he was "born tired."

But much of the fatigue that is in evidence today is not physical but functional. It is not due to the fact that we work so hard, but it grows out of an attitude toward that work. It is not so much in the muscles as in the mind.

This does not imply that mental fatigue is easier to bear. All fatigue, whether psychic or physical, leads to a lack of efficiency and a sort of low and depressed feeling. But, in the healthy person, such fatigue is easier to overcome, and it does not require the kind of tonics that you take out of a bottle. It merely requires a change in mental attitude.

TIREDNESS CAN BE MENTAL

You have most likely had the experience that you came home from work at the close of day feeling thoroughly exhausted. You said, "How glad I am to be home! I'm just going to sit down and relax and turn in early for the night." But after a few minutes one of your friends called and invited you to go with them to some place of activity which you enjoy very much. After a little protesting, you go out, enjoy the evening, and you never think of your fatigue again. All the symptoms have suddenly disappeared.

Such tiredness displays an attitude of the mind rather than an aching back. Your mental approach to your work makes all the difference. If your work makes you tense, or if you feel yourself driven by your superiors, you will find that you will become far more tired than you should.

That tired feeling often arises out of discontent. If you dislike your work, or feel that it is boring, it will make you weary. I can remember that when I was a boy I would become extremely tired when I had to mow the lawn or weed the garden; but, somehow or other, a ball game that required far more physical energy, did not bother me at all.

ORGANIC FACTORS

To be sure, there is also organic fatigue. Our bodies do get tired, even Jesus was wearied at times. When we do not get enough sleep, when we have to be active for a long period of time, or when muscles have to be used for some length of time, there is physical fatigue. It is a blessing that it is so, for this is a call to rest ourselves so that we will not strain our muscles too severely. The Lord has graciously provided sleep and rest to overcome it.

Tension, grief, and disappointment can also cause extreme fatigue. This may be so severe that a person becomes incapacitated for work and needs medical care to overcome it. Those who suffer from depressions often complain of extreme tiredness. Fortunately, medical help is available for these conditions.

But much of the tired feeling of which we speak is neither of this extreme nature, nor of a physical nature. It is a case of mental attitude. This is something that we can and should overcome.

REMEDIES

If your tired feeling is due to your attitude towards your daily work, try taking a different attitude. Work, even the most menial of tasks, need not be drudgery. In fact, it is not the kind of work you do that makes it drudgery; it is your emotional approach. For some people, scrubbing a floor can be done to the tune of a song; to others, preaching a sermon may be sheer drudgery. It all depends upon your attitude.

A pessimistic outlook upon life often leads to fatigue; in fact it makes one tired to be in the presence of a pessimist. A more optimistic viewpoint gives courage and strength even when adversity comes. A worrisome approach can make the day seem long, and the nights even longer, and gives little hope for rest.

To overcome these feelings we need a higher perspective in life. We must learn to see our work as a means to higher goals. A mother must not just wash dishes, scrub floors, and cook meals; but she is called to provide a home where children may be reared for time and eternity. A father does not just work a machine or run a business; but he is providing for those he loves.

If you think of your work in that light, it will remove somewhat of the feeling of drudgery or the tired feeling, and it will fill you with higher incentives that drive you. It is for this reason also that our Lord breaks the routine and monotony of the week, by setting aside the first day of the week as a day of rest. This is not just physical rest, but mental and emotional rest that gives a driving force for the days of the week.

For He still calls the "weary and heavyladen" unto himself and promises, "I will give you rest."

29. Feelings of Guilt

We are all confronted by many conflicts in life. One of the greatest of these is the conflict between good and evil, between right and wrong. This has been going on ever since man sinned and hid himself, out of shame, in the trees of the garden of Eden. Living in the stream of humanity, none of us can really escape this conflict and struggle. For we find sin in our hearts, in our minds, and in our actions and attitudes. It is when we become aware of these sins in us that we have feelings of guilt.

There are two kinds of guilt feelings: healthy ones and unhealthy ones. Generally when we speak of a guilt complex we are thinking of an unhealthy guilt. This is an inordinate feeling of guilt, the kind we often meet in a depressed person. You see it in a person who feels that he has sinned so deeply that there is no place of forgiveness. In extreme cases such people feel that they have committed the unpardonable sin.

NEUROTIC GUILT

It is regrettable that people often confuse the sick feelings of guilt with the healthy ones. There are unrealistic, psychological guilt feelings which cannot be resolved simply by confession and the assurance of forgiveness. To come to people who have these sick guilt feelings with the promises of forgiveness is as useless as trying to cure pneumonia in the same way, for these individuals have an illness in the emotional life which makes it impossible for them to take hold of the forgiving love of Christ, much as they would desire it or seek for it.

Deeply burdened souls who say, "I'm afraid that I have committed the unpardonable sin" are emotionally ill. They can never have committed the sin that is described in Matthew 12. If they had committed that sin, they would never feel sorrow for it, nor would they seek for a way of escape. Often a series of electro-tonic treatments will relieve these symptoms. When the symptoms are gone, these people can again enjoy forgiveness and the peace of soul they so earnestly seek.

GENUINE GUILT

But not all guilt feelings are of this nature. There are many people who have real feelings of guilt. It is surprising, when we get an intimate look into the lives of people, how many there are who live with unresolved guilt feelings. They often feel miserable, lack real peace of soul, and may even have various physical complaints due to inner feelings of guilt.

David describes this condition in his own life beautifully. He tells us what went on within his soul when he tried to hide his guilt from himself and from others. "When I kept silence, my bones wasted away through my groaning all day long. For day and night Thy hand was heavy upon me; my strength was dried up as by the heat of summer." Covering up sin, trying to hide it from God and man, trying even to conceal it from our own consciousness, is a dangerous business. It leads to most unhealthy conditions and breaks out in a variety of symptoms in a person's life. It has incapacitated a good many people. It takes its toll in emotional and mental stress.

We frequently see that patients do not seem to recover from their illness until they get their sins off their minds. The mind can be so haunted by memories of past sins—moral indiscretions, acts of dishonesty, secret hostilities—that these become like a deep and festering cancer in the emotional life.

UNCOVERING HIDDEN GUILT

It is for this reason that psychiatrists and pastoral counselors often probe into the background of a person's life. Their purpose is not to dig up all the mire that lies hidden there. But it is a known psychological fact that when these things are brought out into the open the person can find release. Such confession can often be the turning point in a person's recovery.

This is a fact that is receiving far greater emphasis today in psychological circles. It has long been known that the fact of sin has been too great for man to grope with. But today more than ever psychiatrists must deal with the problem of sin and guilt. This is not a simple problem, and there is not a simple solution for it.

When a person has normal feelings of guilt, the only way of escape is to humbly confess the sin, to seek forgiveness and to strive to find the assurance of the accepting love of God. This will require a firm determination to overcome the sin, and as much as possible to right the wrongs that have been brought about by the sin.

But when there are pathological feelings of guilt, the answer is not that simple. People who have these feelings may have tried a hundred times to find release from the load of guilt by confession, but they could not find it. They may need the support and guidance of a psychiatrist, psychologist or trained counsellor. They must be led to an insight into their true condition, must learn to see the relationship between their inner feelings and their emotional conflicts. It is not until such insight has been gained that they are ready to accept forgiveness.

THE GREAT REMEDY

Even in such cases it is still true that there is but one great remedy for sin. That is one place where psychiatrist and pastor can work together to bring relief to a troubled soul. Jesus saw this in the life of the paralytic who was brought to him. He first said to him, "Son, Thy sins be forgiven thee." Then he said "But that ye may know that the Son of Man has power to forgive sin, I say unto thee, arise, take up thy bed and walk." It is this that brings true wholeness, healing of both body and soul.

In my experience I have often met people who find it hard to experience the joy of forgivenesss because they have not really learned to forgive themselves. They cannot get rid of their feelings of guilt, and they are punishing themselves because of their past sins. These sins can fester within them. This is also a deep-seated problem that requires careful and earnest examination.

If God is able to forgive us, should we then not also be able to forgive ourselves? Forgiveness must be practiced as well as received. It is the gift of God's marvelous love, but it requires that we take hold of it and believe it with all our hearts.

I love the story of the return of the prodigal. The father did not say to the returning wanderer, "We'll put you on probation for a while, and see how things go." He freely forgave him all, and as he embraced him he said, "This, my son." The past sin was wiped away completely.

To find real wholeness we need that healing power, the atoning work of Christ, that removes our sins and cleanses from all unrighteousness.

This is the kind of wholeness that leads to real Christian mental health.

30. Feelings of Loneliness

This world is a busy place. There are millions of people rushing from place to place. Our highways are over-crowded with a ceaseless flow of traffic, and thousands of feet beat upon the sidewalks of busy cities. There are always people, and yet more people.

But there are also those who feel alone in the midst of the throng. There is possibly no feeling that is more disheartening than that of loneliness. It was this that called forth the lament of the Psalmist, "No man careth for my soul."

Many of the plaintive songs of today speak of this feeling of aloneness. Much of romantic modern music, the pessimistic negro spiritual and even the croon of western songs, sings out the cry of loneliness. It is a strange paradox in the light of today's discussions about overpopulation.

WHEN HUMAN TIES ARE BROKEN

There are perhaps no words that speak of a deeper hurt in the heart than the words that pastors often hear when a beloved wife or husband has been taken away. "Now I am alone, I must face tomorrow with no intimate loved one to share my joys and sorrows."

A famous author lost his wife while he was writing the book that was to be his major contribution to his field. When it was published he received the plaudits of his co-workers. But he answered, "Since she is gone, I have no one with whom to share my success."

These are real feelings of being alone. And yet, unrelieved and longlasting feelings such as these are unhealthy and unnecessary. Loneliness can be a great danger to us, it can rob us of the needed energies and ambitions for work. It can lead to many temptations. We need not, and we may not remain in such a state.

LONELINESS IS A SYMPTOM

Actually, loneliness is not a condition, it is a symptom. Anyone can feel lonely, even in a crowd of people or in a busy family. There are people who live among others, and yet walk alone. Basically, it is a reaction to life, one that is not healthy. To overcome it we must begin by taking a healthy attitude toward self and our relationship to others.

The solitary person often takes a sour attitude toward life. He is unhappy in the world. He is often not really friendly to himself.

He does not ask, "Why do I feel lonely?" but he will tend to argue that other people are unfriendly. Much loneliness is self-induced. In fact, many people prefer to be that way and do little to overcome it.

TO HAVE A FRIEND, BE A FRIEND

I am sure that a pastor will frequently have this experience in an afternoon of calling on the members of his church. He will visit a widow who lives alone, possibly not in the best of health, but when asked, "Are you ever lonely?" she will say, "No, I have so many friends that I never get a chance to feel lonely."

As he calls in another home where there are similar circumstances, the very first complaint will be, "I feel so lonely, no one ever pays any attention to me." What is the difference between the two? The one has learned the art of friendship, the other has not.

Often older unmarried people tend to feel left out and alone. Many of us know one who has spent all her days unmarried, and in blindness. Her radiant testimony always is, "I have so many friends that I have never had a lonely day." To have a friend, you must be a friend, and you must cultivate friendship. For there is no flower that withers on the vine of neglect sooner than that of friendship.

To be sure, the church has sometimes neglected the lonely. This is a sad indictment against any Christian community. For there is no finer place to find friendship and companionship than in the church and its many organizations. Besides this, there are also clubs for people who have similar hobbies that tend to break down the feeling of aloneness.

HELPING OTHERS

If you feel lonely, remember that there are others who feel far more lonely. Take an interest in helping others. It is not often that we see a lonely doctor, a lonely minister, or a lonely nurse or teacher. Their lives are devoted to helping others, and hence they do not live in solitude.

One of the most powerful means of overcoming the feelings of aloneness is to practice the companionship of God. Our Lord often reached out His hand of blessing to those who walked alone. Cultivate a living, personal friendship with the Friend of sinners and you will always have a Friend.

There is a cure for loneliness in Christ. When you find that, you will never walk alone, no, not even in the valley of the shadows.

31. Don't Step on My Toes

I am sure that all of us have friends and acquaintances whose feelings are very easily hurt. We must always be on our guard since they are overly-sensitive to the slightest remark that is made. We can never feel quite comfortable in their presence.

Sometimes we find situations that develop in a home because both husband and wife are overly-sensitive. Their relationship is that of two people who both say, "Don't you dare to step on my toes." It leads to constant conflict over many real or imagined insults. It may even be a gesture or an attitude that keys off this hurt feeling.

HURT FEELINGS

Why are some people so sensitive? In dealing with such persons you will usually find that they are people with a feeling of inner insecurity and inferiority. A person who is strong and confident will not be easily threatened by others. But when they are uncertain in themselves and not too confident about their own abilities, they will be easily hurt by the criticisms and remarks of others.

Such persons are living on the defensive. They take a "boxer's stance" to their fellows. There is a feeling of uneasy pride, for they too want to succeed in life. But the least obstacle that is thrown in their way and that threatens their progress will make them feel insulted.

I suppose this spirit is learned in childhood. It can well be caused by rivalries with brothers or sisters in the family. Parents can encourage this by telling them that the neighbor's boy does things much better than their own boy, or that a cousin is much more of a success, and then ask, "Why can't you be like that?" This helps to develop a feeling of inferiority.

REMEDIES

Various suggestions have been made as to how to remove these hurt feelings. A good one is to go to the person who has hurt your feelings and tell him about it. Tell him how you feel. You may find out that no insult was intended, and that you were quite mistaken about the person's attitude. Another suggestion is that when your feelings have been hurt, you should write a letter to the person, tell him what he has done, and frankly express how you feel about it. Then take the letter and tear it into little pieces and throw it away.

Such methods may help for a time to remove the hurt feeling. But they will not prevent you from having more hurt feelings tomorrow. Some people I know would be writing a lot of letters, if they used that means. This would only be treating the symptoms, not the sickness itself.

Basically, it is a weakness that lies deeper in the personality. We need to sit down and carefully examine ourselves. Try to find out why we are on the defensive and why are we so easily threatened? Try to get at the source of the matter.

If you can't do this alone, talk it over with some trusted friend, or your pastor, or a professional counsellor.

OTHERS ARE HUMAN TOO

In all our relationships with others we must know that others are human too. It is strange that an overly-sensitive person can often administer stinging insults to others. They can step on other people's toes, but they guard their own toes with great zeal.

If we are really honest with ourselves we would confess that many of the things that give hurt feelings, hurt us so much because they are, at least in part, true. We have accused ourselves of the same things, but when others tell us, we become angry and hostile.

THE REAL SOLUTION

It is good to examine ourselves as to why we are so sensitive to the touch of others. Why are we on the defensive? Is it possible that there are shortcomings that we are not willing to admit to ourselves and that we fear will not be detected by others?

It is inspiring to hear David speak of this in Psalm 139. He has just said, "Do I not hate them, O Jehovah, that hate Thee?" Then he looks at himself, and begins to use the personal pronouns "Me" and "My." "Search me, O God, and know my heart; try me, and know my thoughts."

If you think someone has hurt you, pray the prayer of David earnestly and I am sure that you will rise to your feet and find the hurt feeling gone.

32. Overcoming Jealousy

There are few of us who have not at times felt the pangs of jealousy. This is a very common emotion among children and can cause many unwholesome rivalries in the home and family. But many people who have reached mature years still indulge in their jealous moods.

It must be evident that not all jealousy is evil. God is described as a jealous God, which means that He demands our exclusive loyalty, because He is the sovereign God. Paul says of the church, "I have been jealous over you with godly jealousy." This means that he is very solicitous for the welfare of the church.

It is a worthy trait of character to desire the wholehearted love of those whom we love and to be solicitous over their welfare. But when this love-protective jealousy is carried to an extreme, it leads to serious consequences. No jealous person can be truly happy. He may have far greater blessings than others do, but if his heart is jealous he cannot enjoy his blessings or use them aright.

RESULTS OF JEALOUSY

Jealousy is something that incites a person to the most heartless deeds. It often breeds hatred and spite. It makes a person small, mean and capable of serious deceptions. Many anonymous letters have been written by such people. Often such letters will state, "If you knew what I know about her and her family, you would have nothing to do with her." Such innuendos can undermine the good name of a person.

There are frequent examples of jealousy among children in a family. Psychologists like to talk about sibling rivalries. Such rivalries are excited when a child feels that the parents show more attention and love to one child than they do for the other. Maybe one of the girls got a new coat while the other one did not. The girl who did not get the coat will not admit that she is jealous of her sister, but she will show her jealousy by suspicion, by saying mean things to her or about her.

There is often a great deal of jealousy in the years of courtship. A young man takes out a young lady of his choice. But another young lady would also like to have this young man as her own. She can hardly go to the young man and admit this feeling. But she can find fault with the other girl, or try to undermine the confidence of the young man in her. This is often done on the basic assumption that all is fair in love and war. But is it?

In every family circle there are often jealousies among the family members. If one of the in-laws happens to have a better home or a better car than the others, often the green-eyed monster raises its ugly head. Usually the members of the family would not admit that they are jealous, but they express their suspicions in various indirect ways. This may lead to the evil of slander and malicious insults.

SUSPICION

Jealousy and suspicion always go together. The one does not exist without the other. This can be especially serious in the family, for instance, when a wife is jealous of her husband's working with other girls in the office or plant. Frequently this leads on to suspicions which are often entirely unfounded. Or, a husband may be over-possessive of his wife, so that he will hardly trust her in the presence of other men. The searching of husband's pockets by their wives for signs of disloyalty is far more common than many suppose.

A very common form of jealousy is professional jealousy. This is present in all professions. When a teacher tells of all the weaknesses of a fellow teacher, you can be sure that this spirit is revealed in such remarks.

Two friends were living side by side. The one was always watching to see who would come to visit her neighbor. If it was someone she knew, she would be rather upset about it and then would invite the same person to her home. In order to make an impression she would try to excel her neighbor in serving lavish refreshments. She would also use such occasions to say unfavorable things about her neighbor.

I cite this illustration to show to what extremes some will go. The danger involved is that such extreme jealousy borders on rather serious mental illness. When a person feeds such a jealous disposition, there is danger of slipping into a paranoid condition. In such a state people become inordinately suspicious; they are very hard to live with in society and frequently need psychiatric help. Learn to overcome your jealous moods, for they are fraught with both mental and spiritual danger.

CAUSES OF JEALOUSY

Why are people jealous of others? Jealousy is first of all an indication of serious emotional immaturity. A little child is jealous of any rival. As the child becomes older he must learn to overcome such jealous feelings. This is something that parents must instil within children as they develop.

Another reason for feelings of jealousy is basic insecurity and inferiority. A little girl is jealous of her sister because she feels that her parents give the sister more advantages or that she has certain qualities that she herself does not possess. A young man marries a very popular girl in the church, knowing that other men would have liked to marry her. Because of his own feelings of insecurity he does not trust her in the company of other men. A person that is not able to trust others is usually not too trustworthy himself. A man who does not trust his wife does not feel too confident about his own faithfulness. For we all tend to judge others by ourselves. We see others in the light of ourselves.

CONQUERING JEALOUS MOODS

The first step in conquering jealousy is to determine why we feel that way. Try to determine the cause of this morbid and dangerous emotion. When you find the root of it, get rid of it.

But to really overcome it will require that we develop a sense of maturity in our life. Paul tells us to overcome evil with good. Learn to overcome envying and jealousy by learning to trust others. We cannot live in married life if we do not learn to trust our marriage partner. You cannot live in society if you do not learn to trust your fellowmen.

One of the best ways to conquer the evil of jealousy in our lives is to learn to conquer our own spirit. For only in that measure can we live in a happy and blessed relationship with others.

Jesus taught us the way. It is to practice the spirit of love for our fellowmen, love that is hallowed by our love for Him. For in that love there is no room for jealousy or suspicion. "A new commandment I give unto you that ye love one another, even as I have loved you."

33. Our Hidden Resentments

The human mind is like an iceberg, we are told, with only a small part of it showing above the surface. The part that is evident is our conscious mind, that part over which we have control. But we are not fully aware of the unconscious part. Many strong desires and feelings lie hidden there, and these feelings come to expression in our lives in many ways.

The same thing applies to our resentments. We have open resentments that we often frankly express. In this land of plenty we tell others that there are certain foods that we "just can't stand." Although we are less frank to admit it, we often have the same reaction to certain types of people. We dislike them and try to avoid them.

REPRESSED FEELINGS

But far more dangerous to our emotional and spiritual well-being are the hidden or repressed resentments. These may go back many years in our lives, or they may be caused by more recent wounds. Resentment is defined as a feeling of displeasure or indignation that develops from a sense of being injured or offended.

This bitter spirit may be due to a serious frustration. People have a feeling that they have not received their just due from life. Others have received promotions while they were passed by. Others seem to be more prosperous than they are. There may be disappointments in family life, childlessness or the birth of a handicapped child, or the fact that children become delinquent; all these can lead to a feeling of resentment.

It must be emphasized that it is not the experience itself, but the attitude that is taken towards the experience that makes a person bitter. It is true, others may have hurt us and done great harm, but this is not a justifiable excuse for resentment. In fact, resentment can be explained but never excused.

HOW EXPRESSED

Resentment expresses itself in various ways. Some people will manifest a hostile attitude when you are first introduced to them. Others show very strong likes and dislikes and are not afraid to express them. Usually, people who are critical of others harbor some resentment. Some people will even show hostilities toward the whole social structure, or towards the church.

Often these resentments will express themselves in physical symptoms. If you take resentments to bed with you, you are going to have trouble sleeping. Sometimes headaches, digestive disturbances, and other bodily symptoms will be seen. Frequently the alcoholic has deep resentments. Many accidents are caused by those who harbor feelings of hostility.

Such feelings are not reserved for older people; they are also evident in the spirit of rebellion shown by children and young people. Much of the cynical and hostile attitude towards authority, towards parents and teachers, reveals resentment.

Naturally, this spirit can cause its greatest harm in the family circle. When frequent quarrels break out, or when a member of the family becomes hard to live with, you can almost be sure that there are these repressed feelings of inner displeasure. For the resentful person is always unhappy.

OVERCOMING HOSTILITY

It is not easy to overcome a hostile feeling when its real cause is hidden. Most people will not allow open hatred to linger long in their lives. But when such hatred is hidden, we often are not aware of our own inner feelings.

It is important to try to find out why we react in such a hostile way. When did this feeling start? What caused it? If you cannot trace your feeling of resentment to its origin, talk it over with a trusted friend or with your pastor. When you find the real cause of your resentment, you can do much to relieve your own feelings and to improve your relations with others.

But a better way is not to allow these resentments to develop. Jesus tells us to learn to forgive our fellowmen "from the heart." Paul tells us not to let the sun go down on our wrath. Sir William Osler advises "to undress our souls at night." When we really do this before God, we cannot harbor resentments in our hearts.

If we will realize that we live in a world of sinners, or at best imperfect Christians, and that there are bound to be hurts in life, it will help much to control our inner feelings. Yes, we will hurt others, and others will at times hurt us. There will be injustices in life. But recognizing our own imperfections as well as the sins of others, we can bow before a holy God and earnestly pray each day, "Father, forgive us our debts, as we also forgive our debtors." There is no room for resentment there.

It is difficult to know how to measure degrees of suffering, but those who know tell us that there is no greater suffering than that of an acute depression. Even in its milder forms it incapacitates a person from constructive work. It creates the feeling of hopelessness and worthlessness.

Dr. J. D. Mulder, our senior consulting staff psychiatrist at Pine Rest, has without doubt seen more people in depressions than any man in this community. For more than forty years he has been dealing with them. In the introduction to a pamphlet entitled *Essays on Mental Disturbance and Demon Possession* he gives a clear-cut description of a person in a state of depression.

> The early symptoms of this condition, which may arise gradually or be sudden in their onset, present a patient as it were engulfed in an abyss of gloom and despair. There is a marked change in the sensorium. Impressions received through the senses become unpleasant and even painful. The eye dreads the daylight, the ear considers the song of the bird or the laughter of the child unbearable. A perversion of the sense of taste and smell may result in the abhorrence of the most delicious food and drink, and the touch of the softest garment leaves an irritating impression.

Depressions may range in severity from mild feelings of despondency to a grave mental illness. A depression may be a short and fleeting mood swing, or an extremely obstinate and vicious condition. All of us swing in our moods—we have our highs and lows—but in depression a person swings to depths beyond the normal level, and since he cannot help himself to get out he feels that all is lost.

SEEKING PROFESSIONAL HELP

It is quite evident that not every depression need drive us to see a psychiatrist or professional counselor. In many cases it is something that will pass away, and we need not be too alarmed about it.

But when there is a deep depression, one that persists, it is well to seek help. In fact, it is much better to seek psychiatric help before the depression becomes too deep-set and chronic. Waiting too long can be both costly and dangerous.

It is much like treating a cold. If the ordinary home remedies do not cure the cold, you go to see a doctor. In many cases of depression the family doctor can be of assistance, and usually he will be able to detect whether you need to see a psychiatrist or not. Today, much can be done to alleviate this condition, and it is the course of wisdom to use these means.

HOME REMEDIES

There are certain home remedies that you can apply when you feel depressed. There are certain rules that can be followed:

When you feel depressed it is good to keep busy. It is not to your advantage to sit down and worry about it. Nor does it help for a relative or friend to tell you to snap out of it. Get busy with something that diverts your attention. If your regular work does not keep you busy, find something to do around the house. Sedentary brooding merely encourages depression. That is one of the reasons for the use of various activity programs at mental hospitals today. Busy hands can do much to get our minds back into a normal mood.

This does not mean that we would discourage thinking. Idle thinking is to be shunned, because it leads to self-pity. Constructive thinking can be an emotional tonic. I know of a man who found help by solving difficult mathematical problems. Others find it in reading a good book. Still others find help in taking a trip.

I would not encourage reading books on how to overcome worry and how to conquer your fears. There are many of these books on the market, but most of them are written for people who are emotionally well. They are not wholesome for the depressed, who are emotionally sick.

A DEPRESSION IS A LIE

Actually, a depression is a lie. When a person is driven by the prevailing winds of discouragement and melancholy, he is telling himself that he is worse than he actually is. A depressed man feels that all is hopeless. But this is an untruth. As long as there is life, there is also hope. In this world nothing is really hopeless. Dante tells us that over the gates of hell there is the inscription "Abandon hope, all ye that enter here." That is the only place we may call hopeless.

A depression looks at life with dark glasses. The past is dark, and so are the present and the future. The sins of the past loom up large, and there seems to be no forgiveness for them.

When life is viewed in that way, it is little wonder that a depressed person feels so hopeless that he considers suicide as the only way of escape. This is one of the real dangers of a serious depression.

A well-balanced person does not allow himself to be swayed by his emotions. He allows his intellect to guide his feelings, his reason to control his emotions. These two elements are also found in the Christian faith. Faith is knowledge, but also trust. In a depression the knowledge part remains, but the trust part seems to fail. For the trust part is emotional, and this is where a depression strikes.

A REASONED HOPE

A depression tells us that there is no hope. But the Christian faith tells us that hope remains firm and sure. Hope is the dominant characteristic of the Christian spirit and experience. Place then over against the hopelessness of a depression a reasoned hope—a hope that is built upon the faithfulness of God, upon His gracious promises, and the atoning work of the Savior.

I find that a passage of Scripture that gives great strength and help, at least for the moment, is found in Philippians 1:6: "He who began a good work in you will perfect it until the day of Jesus Christ."

SPIRITUAL THERAPY

David in Psalm 42 and 43 made use of excellent spiritual therapy. Three times in these two psalms he sinks into depressed and hopeless feelings, and he says "Why art Thou cast down, O my soul, and why art thou disquieted within me?" And the answer comes back to him, as he speaks to his own soul, "Hope thou in God, who is the help of my countenance, and my God." He does this a second time, as a wave of depression again strikes. And then a third time. And this final word in Psalm 43 is, "Who is the health of my countenance." Such hope gives healing.

William Cowper was a man who struggled much with despondency. He made several attempts to take his own life. One of his biographers writes "Let those who are assailed by despondency remember that William Cowper lived to write:

> 'God moves in a mysterious way,
> His wonders to perform.
> He plants his footsteps on the seas,
> and rides upon the storm.' "

35. Your Nerves and You

In everyday speech we frequently talk about being "nervous." Mrs. Jones is called "a bundle of nerves." General practitioners will often examine a patient, find nothing physically wrong, and say, "It's just your nerves."

There is not much objection to the use of these terms, provided we understand them properly. It sounds a lot more respectable to have a "nervous breakdown" than to suffer from a "manic-depressive psychosis" or a "psycho-neurosis." We should allow the person who suffers from these conditions to describe them in his own terms.

NERVOUSNESS NOT PHYSICAL

But it is important to know that nervousness is not a disease of the nerves. When we say that we are nervous and high-strung, we do not mean to say that our physical nerves are actually stretched tight. No more, for instance, than we mean an actual, physical pain when we say that someone gives us a pain in the neck.

The cause of nervousness is not in the nervous system as such. A person may be so nervous that he needs care in a mental hospital and still have a healthy nervous structure. Actual organic disease of the nervous system can be readily detected by a neurologist. If a nerve is injured in one form or another, it will be detected in the functioning of the system. If a nerve is cut by a knife, it will not cause nervousness, but paralysis of the muscles controlled by that nerve.

Nervousness is found in the presence of a nervous system that is healthy. There are other causes for such a condition. A student taking a final examination may feel nervous. He may have palpitations of the heart and strange feelings in his stomach.

We have little exact knowledge about the cause of nervousness, for it is manifest in many diverse and complicated ways. Most of us are familiar with the experience, for almost all people will be nervous at one time or another. Naturally, some are far more nervous than others.

SOLUTIONS

For many this is not a serious problem. It comes and goes and does not hinder greatly in the regular routine of life. But for others it can be a serious handicap under certain circumstances in life. When nervousness does become a serious problem, it is difficult to cope with. All the remedies of well-meaning friends and relatives may be quite useless. There are no easy solutions. Many are reluctant to seek help, and they suffer in proud secrecy.

BREAKING DOWN IN CRISES

The nervous person usually becomes confused and fearful when he comes face to face with an emotional crisis. He will be sure that the worst is going to happen to him, and this may drive him into panic. The panic makes the emotional disturbance worse, so the result will be even greater panic. The cycle will go on until he finds some way to get hold of himself and to break the cycle.

Our greatest need is to gain insight into this condition. Try to discover the cause of it by tracing it back to its earliest beginnings. For, basically, these conditions arise in the emotional life in the process of the developing personality. As a rule, the cause will be emotional.

It is often hard for us to delve into the problem of our own nervousness, and we may need the help of others to overcome it. This some are reluctant to do. A brilliant person whom I have seen a few times found it difficult to accept help from someone whose IQ rating was twenty points lower than his. But he forgot that the powers of inner analysis are limited when we are emotionally upset.

AN EMOTIONAL PROBLEM

Since the problem of nervousness is basically an emotional one, people who are nervous will often have spiritual conflicts. It is only natural that this condition would also affect the spiritual emotions. This involvement can make our nervousness even more painful, for at such a time we especially need the resources of our faith.

When a person gains insight into himself, he will find that the ultimate resources of his spiritual life can help him gain stability and strength. A silent prayer can keep a person from slipping into panic. But this is only possible when faith in God permeates all the recesses of a man's life, including his emotional life.

36. Accentuating Our Successes

For all of us there are moments of success as well as moments of failure. No person ever has success 100 per cent of the time, nor does a person fail in every attempt in life. It is well for us to learn that this is so. The failures in life help us to be humble, while the successes keep us from utter discouragement. To live healthy lives we must learn to live in the light of our best accomplishments and not in the shadow of our defeats.

Have you ever watched a young child learn to walk? He first takes a faltering step and fails, often wailing with indignation because he has failed. But, with a little encouragement, he soon tries again, he takes one step and then another, and so learns to walk. Each successful step is an encouragement to him, and so he builds up his confidence.

Some people tend to accentuate their failures. We all have them, but it makes a world of difference how we view them. If a young bride would feel frustrated by her first failures in baking and cooking, she would never learn to be a good homemaker. If a fisherman would give up fishing as a sport just because he failed to obtain a good catch, there would be very few men interested in this hobby.

I am sure that every minister conducts a service that does not go as well as he had planned. The sermon does not seem to flow too well, the congregation is restless, and so he leaves the church building with a feeling of discouragement. This may well lead to a blue Monday, but it should not lead to blue Tuesday and Wednesday.

It happens in families that there are several fine sons and daughters, but there is one who is not a credit to the family ideals. Often parents tend to brood about this one failure to the point of forgetting the blessing that their family has been to them. This is accentuating a failure and minimizing success.

The trouble with this attitude is that we tend to concentrate on our liabilities, on the things we have not been able to accomplish, and thus we lose sight of the real perspective of living. It is dangerous to develop a feeling that we must always succeed. This stems from an inner pride. We forget that we are human. Other people have failures, should not we expect them too?

LEARNING FROM OUR FAILURES

Failures do have a place in life. They should teach us to search out where we have made our mistakes and why we have not accomplished what we set out to do. And then we must learn from these mistakes so that we may be able to do better in the future.

The scientists in their experiments have seldom gained success in their early attempts. Thomas Edison made more than four hundred models that failed before he successfully developed the incandescent lamp. Madame Curie worked in great difficulties and with many failures before she found Radium. All scientific development has come by learning from failures. It is not the failure that is important, it is the attitude we take towards it.

The ten spies who spied out the land of Canaan made an interesting statement when they said, "We seemed in our eyes as grasshoppers in their sight." This was a confession of a feeling of failure and defeat.

Failure keeps us humble, but it must not paralyze us from further effort. We must learn to do what Paul tells us to do, "Forgetting the things which are behind, and stretching forward . . . I press on . . ."

FACING SUCCESS

There is a perfectionism that is unwholesome. That is the one in which we feel defeated because we have not reached a perfect state. This has led many people to discouragement and even depression.

But there is also a desire for perfection that is good. We may not set our goals too low. We may not say, "Well, others fail, it's not so bad that I fail too." We must rise up from our failures and face success. This must be our goal — to do things in the best possible way. And each one of us can gain success in some small way in life.

There is also a variety of gifts, but all have some gifts that they can use. No one of us is so devoid of resources that we cannot live creatively in some area of life. In the human symphony there is room also for the smaller instruments. In this matter we must be content to be ourselves, but to do this in the best possible way.

Live then in the light of your successes and do not dwell in the shadow of your failures. This is true also in our spiritual lives. We must not be forever fretting about past sins, but we must rise to move ahead creatively in Christian living.

This would help us to get rid of some of this morose deadness, and to move forward into the bright sunlight of successful living. That is, living victoriously, because we confess belief in a Victorious Christ.

HANDLING OUR TENSIONS AND ANXIETIES

But if God doth so clothe the grass of the field,
which today is,
and tomorrow is cast into the oven,
shall he not much more clothe you,
O ye of little faith?

Be not therefore anxious, saying,
what shall we eat?
or, What shall we drink?
or, Wherewithal shall we be clothed?

But seek ye first his kingdom,
and his righteousness;
and all these things shall be added unto you.

— Jesus, in Matthew 6:30-33

37. Living in a Time of Tension

Walking up and down State Street in Chicago, Fifth Avenue in New York, Monroe Avenue in Grand Rapids or Main Street in any town, it is interesting to study the faces of the people who move restlessly by. It is soon evident that there are very few of them that have a relaxed and composed look. There are lines of concern, of hurry and worry, of anxiety and tension. It has almost become trite to say that this is an age of tension.

In a way, it is surprising that it is so. Actually, we live far more comfortably than did our parents and grandparents. Modern mechanization has made our daily work much easier. Social security, hospitalization insurance, and old-age assistance have provided us with protective measures for almost all of life's emergencies.

And yet, we are more tense. You can read it on the faces of people, even in church. You see it in the lives of teen-agers, and it seems to form part of the spirit of rebellion that is so common at that age. You can even observe it in men and women on vacation, or when they try to relax on a golf course.

WHY ARE WE TENSE?

Where then does this tension lie? Not first of all in the external circumstances of life, but in the hearts of the people. It is their reaction to life.

In the world in which we live we cannot escape external and situational tensions. We come face to face with conflicts on the national and international levels, in employer-employee relationships, in the social pressures of the age, and in an ever-increasing way in the home and family. There is the struggle for status, and there are many prejudices of race, creed and color.

These are realistic conflicts. Yet I am convinced that the basic tensions of today are not in the external events, but in our own personal reactions to these events. It is not the age that is tense, but we who are living in this age.

The early pioneers who settled in this part of the country had struggles for survival that were far more severe than we can even imagine. There was never enough food; sickness and death were constantly among them. They worked hard from dawn till dusk, but at night they could fold their toil-worn hands and sleep peacefully.

Today the sons and grandsons of these pioneers drive home from air-conditioned offices down spacious expressways; many spend the night in cottages on cool lakes. But when they lie down to sleep they need a sedative or a tranquilizer to relieve their tensions.

TENSIONS ARE REACTIONS

Tensions are reactions. And what an uncomfortable word "tension" is. It makes us think of inability to relax muscles, of the neck and the back becoming rigid and sore. It speaks of sleeplessness due to the pressure of busy thoughts. It is something that tends to paralyze and cripple us in our work.

Unfortunately, it cannot be relieved by the pleasant little pills that are so freely advertised. It requires a good deal more than that.

Tension is also contagious, for a tense person is usually irritable and disagreeable. One tense person in a family can set the whole family on edge, especially if this involves one of the parents. It is like driving in a car with a jittery and excited driver; no one else in the car can relax either.

Tension is something that affects people of all classes. Ministers are subject to it as well as laymen; teachers as well as pupils; the white-collared worker as well as the man that toils with pick and shovel. And today it is affecting people at an earlier age than ever before. The largest number of admissions to mental hospitals today is in the age group of below 45 years of age.

To be sure, there are some tensions caused by illness. They are one of the symptoms of certain emotional and mental disturbances. Some people finally become so tense that they need the care of psychiatrists and mental hospitals.

TAKING OURSELVES TOO SERIOUSLY

But there are far more forms of tension that arise from the fact that people take themselves too seriously. They think so much in terms of self. They often develop a feeling that they are quite indispensable which is a mark of emotional immaturity. They have never really learned to face up to life with its conflicts and frustrations. They have not learned to know themselves.

Usually, we cannot control the external forces of life. We cannot always smooth the path and remove all obstacles. In a highly competitive society there will be conflicts. This we cannot change.

But we can control our *attitude* towards life's struggles. This is something that we should learn as children. It is very important for parents to teach their children that life will require adjustments on our part. Too often we try to shield our children so that they never really learn to face up to life.

HANDLING TENSIONS WISELY

A Christian must learn to handle his tensions wisely. Ultimately you cannot run away from them. You cannot tranquilize yourself by a mere act of the will. But you can press on towards greater emotional and spiritual maturity—for here is the only effective answer.

Jesus saw the lines of tension on the faces of the people who stood before Him, and He tells them "Be Not Anxious." But to overcome tensions, we must do more than just "pray about them."

I think Paul had the answer in his own life. While lying in a prison cell he is able to say "I have learned in whatever state I am, therewith to be content." And he tells us the secret of this contentment: "I know how to be abased, and I know how to abound." In other words, Paul says "I have learned to be unbroken by life's adversities and to be unspoiled by its prosperity." This speaks of both emotional and spiritual maturity.

An old saint who seemed to breathe this spirit of quiet composure shared his secret with others when he said "When I go to sleep at night, I have learned to say from the heart:

> 'Drop Thy still dews of quietness
> Till all our strivings cease.
> Take from our lives the strain and stress
> And let our ordered lives confess,
> Thy beauty and Thy peace.' "

38. Conflicting Desires

Of all our emotional problems possibly none disturbs more of us than nervous tension. Many people, who never read a book, will avidly devour page after page of the more popular books on how to find release from tensions. Almost every nationally known magazine has some article about it. It shows that many people are under pressure.

Nervous tension is a serious thing. It destroys personal happiness and impairs efficiency in work. It ruins family life and disrupts many interpersonal relationships. It has provoked people to write letters they should never have mailed, and to say words that they wish they could revoke. Much of the irritability and disagreeableness of people is caused by it.

A BASIC STRUGGLE

Generally the blame of nervous tension is attributed to the pressure of modern life. It is true that many of the miracles of modern civilization are both a bane and a blessing. But when all this has been said, does this really explain the cause of tensions?

There is one cause that is frequently overlooked, and yet I feel that stands as one of the primary ones. It is the fact that man is divided within himself, that he is at war with himself. Serious tension always implies that there are conflicting desires within the soul. The major conflict is one described in the Bible as the one between "God and Mammon."

Through the redeeming work of Christ, and the indwelling Spirit, the Christian has spiritual goals and aspirations. But in opposition to these, our culture, our environment continually lure us to a materialism which places the physical above the spiritual, things above the person.

These contrary movements in our innermost self tend to tear us apart. It reminds us of a person being tortured on a rack. This was an instrument of torture consisting of rollers on each end to which the limbs were fastened and between which the body was stretched in a most painful way.

This inner struggle also is torture, for there is within us that which would yield to the spiritual desires, and there is also within us that which would give heed to the material. Jesus says flatly, "It can't be done, for no man can serve two masters." Life tells us the same thing through nervous tensions. In the Christian there is that

118

which would honor God as Lord of all of life, but there is also the carnal nature that seeks satisfaction in baser things.

This does not mean that all our tensions are due to ungodliness, or that the true believer will never be afflicted by them. Paul teaches us just the opposite as he describes the struggles in his own soul in Romans 7. Nor will this tension be immediately removed when we surrender ourselves to God.

A LIFE-LONG BATTLE

Giving one's self to God is not a single act, something like laying a ten-dollar bill on the counter. The whole person must be gathered together and surrendered. And this whole person has a past, filled with habits of living. In it there are varying desires that come to us just because we are human. We bring to the Christian faith the kind of person we are, emotionally, mentally, socially and physically.

When the Great Potter is busy remaking the vessel that has been marred on the wheel of life, it takes a lifetime of moulding and fashioning and wrestling. The building of a character takes the entire span of life. Let us not suppose, as so many modern books would suggest, that there is some magic religious potion that can be given that will make all our tensions suddenly evaporate. Such wounds heal slowly. The cleavage in our personality is knitted together only by long and prayerful battle.

We know that God can work more suddenly, and we do not question His ability to make exceptions, but the customary practice is that it takes a long time. God has many lessons to teach us while He is healing the conflicts in the soul.

THE VICTORY

How then can we conquer in this warfare? It requires more than just to watch and pray, although the prayer, "Unite my heart to fear Thy name," has a very real part in it. I feel that we must conquer the spiritual battle in the same way that we conquer the battle over our tensions in everyday living.

To conquer life's tensions we must learn to take one thing at a time. When we are assigned the task of cutting down a forest, we first determine to cut down ten trees a day, and then go at it taking one tree at a time. We must discipline ourselves to so schedule our time that we need not be thinking of doing many things at once, but one thing at a time. This must become a mental attitude. This will lead to a concentration of effort, and of interest.

This is also the remedy in the struggle within. We must come to the point where the Psalmist stood when he said, "One thing have I desired"; or that of Paul when he taught, "One thing I do." We are to put all our variant desires under one greater and larger desire—that we may please Him.

Most of our worries are about material things. We think too much about what is going to happen tomorrow, or next week, but we often forget the larger question of life, "What about eternity?" We see the next step, but how about the distant scene?

When we place all of life in the perspective of eternity, we gain a view that tends to unite it. When we bring all of life under the sway of Christ, even bringing every thought captive to Him, we bring a united heart—a whole life.

During the Civil War a few of the Generals of the Northern Army came to President Lincoln and suggested that it might be better to divide the country and stop the bloodshed. Lincoln placed his large rail-splitter's hand on the map of the United States and said, "It all belongs to the United States, we may not divide it." When we come with our life, torn asunder by many conflicting desires, Christ lays His nail-scarred hand upon it and says, "It all belongs to My Father and your Father."

39. Tension—Your Master, or Your Servant?

There are various ways in which people meet the tensions of which we wrote. The way they face them will depend to a large extent on how they learned to face frustrations in childhood. Some of us as parents have taken the attitude that we do not want our children to have the same struggles in life that we experienced. We try to shield them and give them more protection than is good for them.

HANDLING CONFLICTS

Every child must learn to develop healthy ways of handling conflicts. A child must learn such matters as fair play in his games, he must learn to share what he has with others, he must also learn to be a good loser when the occasion arises. It is not good for a person to have everything handed to him on a silver platter.

If we live on a superficial emotional level, giving vent to our feelings as they come up within us, we have never grown up emotionally. In the process of emotional maturing, we must learn to handle our tensions—or otherwise we become slaves to them.

ESCAPE

Many people try to escape any form of conflict. There are many ways in which people take flight, but everyone of them is an indication of an unhealthy attitude towards life's battles. Some people will transfer tense feelings from the real problem to one that they think they can handle. A man cannot very well speak his mind when he has been criticized by his boss. But when he comes home he can take out his frustrations on his children, or on his wife. They then feel the sting of his hostile feelings.

Others find excuses and alibis. When there is tension in the home because of financial problems, a wife will often blame her husband because he does not give the family enough financial security. The husband will in turn blame his wife because she does not manage finances well and has a poor sense of values.

You cannot escape tensions by trying to run away from them. For you cannot escape yourself. Each person must come to terms with himself. We have tried to show that tension is an inner attitude toward a situation, rather than the situation itself. There will always be areas of external conflicts as long as we live in a world of sinners. But we can do something about these inner feelings and reactions.

For some people, even religion becomes a form of escape. We often meet people who are very tense; you can see it in their bearing, in the way they grip the arms of the chair or the fact that they have their fingernails bitten to the quick. And when you talk to them they say, "I have been praying about it." We surely would not discourage prayer, but we must not expect the Lord to do for us what we should be doing for ourselves. I am also sure that the kind of prayer that is prayed would reveal the same tensions the person has in his life. Our prayers, too, can become tense and worry-filled.

CONTAGIOUS TENSION

Tension not only makes a person unhappy and incapacitates for work, but it is also extremely contagious. A tense person is on edge, easily upset and jittery. And this tends to rub off on the rest of the family. A mother or father who is constantly tense will inadvertanly make the children tense. A tense teacher affects the whole class. A tense foreman will also make the men that work for him tense.

It is especially in the home where the results are felt most deeply. Lasting tensions are most unwholesome for an impressionable child. The seeds for more tension are planted in the generation to follow, and possibly in more than one.

In a following chapter I would like to suggest certain practical suggestions on the matter of getting ourselves from under the slavery of tensions. For to live effectively as Christians, to perform our work well and to set a healthy attitude for the home, we must learn to handle life's tensions constructively.

40. Common-sense Remedies for Tension

There is no simple prescription that can be given with a guarantee that it will relieve tensions. There are books and articles and TV ads that would give that impression. But to overcome tensions is a part of emotional maturing. This cannot be done in 10 easy lessons, for it takes constant self-discipline.

I would like to present a few suggestions that some people have found helpful in handling their tensions. Perhaps they will also be of some help to our readers.

PLAN YOUR DAY, OR YOUR WEEK, SO THAT YOU HAVE A WORKABLE PLAN

Some people make a well-worked-out schedule, allotting a certain amount of time to each task that must be accomplished. We often try to cram too much into a day. Confronted with a day full of varied work, we are distracted and find it hard to get any of the work completed.

It may be of help to write out such a schedule, just as teachers must do in their classrooms. If you do, you may even be able to squeeze in a short nap without feeling guilty. Remember that your schedule must be one that is workable for *you;* no one else can prescribe it for you.

LEARN TO DO ONE THING AT A TIME

A tense person scatters his efforts by trying to do several things at once. While he is doing one task, he is thinking and worrying about the next one, or about the one he forgot to do yesterday. Tension interferes with concentration on the task at hand, makes the work doubly hard, and prevents a person from doing his work well.

Take one step and then another. Do one task, and then take up another. When you are to cut down a forest of trees, you determine to cut down 10 a day, and then you cut down one at time. This requires discipline, but it is worth while.

DO NOT TAKE YOURSELF TOO SERIOUSLY

Learn also to see the lighter side of life. Keep alive your sense of humor, for there is no better safety-valve than a hearty laugh. God gave men the power to weep, but he also gave them the power to laugh. Learn to exercise this gift. Some people say, "Well, what is there to laugh about in a world like this?" If you can't laugh at anything else, laugh at yourself.

It is often easier to laugh when the joke is on somebody else, but we must also learn to laugh when the joke is on us. I am sure that Jesus laughed. There must have been a glint in his eye when He told about the man with a beam in his own eye, trying to flick a speck out of his brother's eye. Who has more right to laugh than a Christian?

LEARN THE ART OF RELAXATION

We need times of relaxation and refreshment in the course of each day. We cannot always keep going at a tense pace. Some people find relaxation while driving their car; others find this a source of added tension. Some find their relaxation on a golf course; others find it in a brisk walk. Some find it in music or painting; others go to a quiet place where there is no telephone to bother them. Some use mechanical gadgets to relax them, although this does seem a bit artificial. Whatever means are best for you, use them to learn to relax.

LEARN TO LIVE AS IN THE PRESENCE OF GOD

It is a bit pathetic to see the overly-conscientious person going about his work as though he is Atlas, carrying the whole world on his shoulders. It is useless to live this way. One day we are going to leave this earth, and it will go on just as well without us. It is a humbling thought, but there are no indispensable men and women. We are here to fulfill our task, to take our place in the succession of history; but one day others will take our place, possibly better than we do it today.

This knowledge challenges us to do our best and to leave the rest in the hands of God, who controls the events from generation to generation. For we are living in a well-ordered world. It may seem topsy-turvy to us at times. But God still rules by all the orderly processes that He has ordained.

So we must live as in the presence of God. The strings of the harp must be drawn tight, so that there may be melody and beautiful harmony. If we are to make music as our Lord intends it, our lives must be drawn to a certain tension. But we must let God do the tuning for us, for it is also his fingers that must pluck the melody from the strings.

41. What Is Anxiety?

There are various words that are used rather indiscriminately. We speak of fear, phobia, tension, and anxiety. In many ways these terms fall into the same category, and yet they are different.

Fear is a response to a threat that is specific and, usually, clearly defined. Fear is basically a healthy emotion, a God-given response to danger. It is a protection for man, since it gives a driving force to get him out of danger. The man who says that he has no fear has only learned to conquer some of his more basic fears.

A phobia is a fear that has become exaggerated and extreme. It is deep-set and hard to overcome. A fear of being shut up in a small place is quite normal, but when one develops claustrophobia, so that he cannot be in a room with a door closed, he has an unreasonable and unhealthy fear.

Anxiety is more vague and diffuse. It is a condition in which we feel threatened in the very foundation of our existence. Rollo May defines anxiety as "a reaction to a threat to the existence of oneself as a human being, or to values that one has identified with his existence." The Holland and German word *angst* describes this feeling very well.

There are actually three levels of anxiety. They are not essentially different and separate, for they often overlap, but they can be distinguished.

NORMAL ANXIETY

Normal anxiety can also be called tension. But tension concerns itself more with conflicts with external objects and persons. Anxiety describes more the inner feelings.

Nothing significant would be performed in life without the aid of some healthy anxiety. This is an emotional stimulus that is helpful. Students who are striving for high academic achievements will be anxious. They have a strong drive to succeed, and a concern that they may fail. It is a good thing that ministers have some anxiety about the worship services of next Sunday; this serves as an incentive to go to the pulpit well prepared.

A girl or boy who is in love has a measure of anxiety. There is always the threat of losing the object of one's affection. In this sense, anxiety is a drive that awakens the best in a person. It helps him to aspire to reach the goals he has, and it instils a fear that he may fail in the attempt. This is a positive and worth-while emotion.

SPIRITUAL ANXIETY

When the soul is driven to the point that man sees himself as a sinner and feels the stinging power of guilt, there is an anxiety that is good. To be sure, such anxiety is most uncomfortable and even painful, but it often serves as an incentive to "drive us trembling to His breast."

The convicting power of the Holy Spirit leads men to a humble confession of sin and a fervent longing for God's saving love. The "broken spirit and the contrite heart" are manifestations of this emotion.

David portrays this beautifully in Psalm 32. "When I kept silence, my bones wasted away through my groaning all the day long. For day and night thy hand was heavy upon me: my moisture was changed as with the drought of summer."

Here too, anxiety serves as an inner incentive. The psychiatrist and the therapist often try to awaken this kind of anxiety in persons with whom they are working. Such an emotion can be most wholesome for them.

NEUROTIC ANXIETY

For some, anxiety serves as a spur that drives them on, for others it becomes a thorn in the flesh that incapacitates them. It can wound and break the spirit of a person. Then anxiety becomes unmanageable and often cannot be relieved without special attention or professional assistance.

We present a few examples to illustrate this fact. When a person observes a growth on the body, some normal anxiety may be justifiable. We have all been warned of the danger of cancer. But when the person goes into hysteria and is incapacitated for work because of this growth, there is evidence of neurotic anxiety. A normal reaction would be to go to a doctor for diagnosis and treatment as promptly as possible.

It is perfectly normal for a hunter in the northern woods to become anxious when he faces a large bear and finds his gun jammed. But it is neurotic when a man is afraid to be in the same room with a house-cat.

A person may be normally serene and confident in life. But when a loved one is suddenly snatched away, he may become withdrawn and depressed, or may go far beyond the normal range of grief. Such anxiety may well be neurotic.

The Christian has an answer to anxiety. I would like to present that answer in another chapter. Meanwhile, it may be well to think of the words of Peter, "Casting all your anxiety upon him, because He careth for you."

42. Our Anxieties and Our Faith

There can be little doubt that there is a close relationship between our faith and the measure of emotional security we enjoy in life. This implies that Christian faith gives us an antidote for anxiety and worry. But the cure for anxiety is not quite as simple as many people would suppose.

There are many who will say to an anxious and troubled person, "Don't worry, just trust more." Others will say, "Just pray about it, and your worries will vanish." These solutions are over-simplifications, and they usually give very little relief.

When a person who is anxious is constantly told that worry is sin, and that it is only a manifestation of a lack of faith, the anxiety may well increase. Then the person will also begin to worry about the fact that he is worrying; he becomes enmeshed in a vicious cycle.

A great deal of unwise emphasis on prayer can also increase anxiety. When a person only prays for relief from worry, but the worry continues, there will be a new worry due to the feeling that the Lord does not answer his prayers.

USING THE MEANS

To gain relief from anxiety we must walk the pathway of prayer and childlike trust, but we must also make use of the means. When you have a toothache you do not only pray for relief; you also visit a dentist. Prayer is of value in every situation of life, but it does not have a direct therapeutic value. If your appendix is inflamed, an operation for appendicitis will accomplish more than a week of prayer. Surgery, here, is God's way of working.

In relieving anxiety, prayer and the use of the means must also go hand in hand. In a deep anxiety state a person may need professional help from a psychiatrist. The psychiatrist may prescribe treatments or medication. It is no disgrace to use such means, nor does it display a lack of faith in God.

I am convinced that in many cases our people are not making adequate use of one of the means the Lord has given us. I am referring to the use of your pastor as a counselor. Many anxious people could find a great deal of relief if they would be willing to talk about their concern to their pastors.

Most of our ministers have some training and experience in

dealing with people who have mild emotional disturbances, and they are eager to serve their parishioners in this way. I have received a good many letters from people, asking for advice that could have been given in a far better way in a personal visit with their own pastor.

SPIRITUAL REMEDIES

One of the reasons why our Christian faith does not help us more is that there is too wide a gap between the truths we confess and the truths by which we live. It is one thing to sing about wonderful peace, but quite another thing to feel that peace. There is often a great deal of difference between our confession of life everlasting and our personal view of death.

Usually, I find that the anxious are both emotionally and spiritually immature. They have need of spiritual growth, as well as of greater emotional stability. These two qualities will often grow together. Such growth can be brought about only by personal exercise of faith in daily life. With some guidance and direction in our devotional life we can grow spiritually, and with such growth there will also be some release from anxiety.

It is true also that an anxious person is usually one who has not learned to forgive himself. He can feel that God has forgiven him his sins, even some of the more evident sins, but he has not really forgiven himself. This leads to feelings of guilt and a need for punishing himself for sins committed. Talking such matters over with an understanding counselor can be of great help.

Usually the anxious person spends too much time thinking about himself. Often he cannot help doing this, for he is deeply conscious of his inner needs. This, too, is something that can be brought into the open by frank discussion. Sometimes the anxious can be helped by entering into some service for others. There is no better way to learn to look away from self than to reach out a helping hand to others who have greater needs than we do.

A vibrant faith in God does offer an antidote for anxiety. The surrendered heart, the dedicated life, the wholehearted trust of the Christian's faith tend to crowd out anxious thoughts and feelings. But the development of such seasoned faith requires effort as well as prayer. This is the only pathway to confident and purposeful living.

43. Flight or Fight

Each of us must face a certain amount of conflict in life. In the kind of world in which we live this is inescapable. But conflict is always a source of discomfort and unhappiness. It brings with it certain tensions, feelings of uneasiness and restlessness. For this reason we all try to resolve our conflicts in one way or another.

Life is a battle. It is a struggle for survival from the womb to the grave. And each of us makes his choice, consciously, or unconsciously, whether he will face the battles with strength or with weakness, whether he will advance to victory or run away in defeat. We can either meet the conflict head-on and fight, or we can try to escape the battle by flight.

Most of us prefer to escape painful realities, for it is normal to try to avoid the unpleasant things of life. The temptation to escape, or to take flight, is common to all of us, and none of us is entirely free from such tendencies.

The desire for self-preservation is a healthy one. It is folly to place ourselves needlessly in danger. It is also perfectly proper to try to improve our position and lot in life. We need not just sit back and "grin and bear it."

But you cannot escape from yourself, nor can you escape the conflicts of life. Each man must come to terms with himself. This will require a choice, one that you cannot escape. You must choose whether you will face up to the battle and fight, or go into retreat and take flight.

ESCAPISM

There are many ways in which people try to run away from conflicts. Some people try to withdraw from the stream of life. The hermits and the monastics of an earlier age attempted this. Today people just withdraw into their own homes. They pull down the shades and turn on TV. In that way they do not have to converse with others, but they can live in the world of unreality of TV commercials and programs.

One man said, "We just don't visit with people anymore; then you never have trouble with them either." This has become somewhat of a socially accepted pattern of behavior in some circles.

Others will take a sort of "mousy" attitude towards life. You can never get into an argument with them, because you can be sure they will never disagree with you. If they have any ideas, they keep them to themselves. This is one way of avoiding conflict, but it is done at the price of weakening the character.

Others have become mental hermits; they either live in caves or in ivory towers, depending upon their viewpoint. They either lift themselves above the stream of men, because they feel superior to the rest, or they retreat into feelings of inferiority and feel that they are not good enough to make a contribution.

A convenient headache can be a marvelous way for some people to escape the conflicts. Others get palpitations around the heart and must avoid all tension-producing difficulties. This is quite acceptable in most social circles.

A girl who found that in her youth she could get her way by shedding a few tears continued to use this same mechanism when she married. These tears still work wonders on her husband, and she has even found them a convenient means of getting out of a traffic ticket.

Some find alcohol as a way of escape from the stinging conflicts and defeats of everyday life. Going off into a stuporous or drunken spree gives only a temporary escape, but it is a very common method. Sleeping pills and tranquilizers can also serve as the same kind of crutch. When the conflicts become too severe, just take one of the wonder working pills, and relief is in sight. Of course, the extreme form of escape is in suicide. In this way the person tries to escape all conflict and to do so permanently.

WHY DO PEOPLE TAKE FLIGHT?

Why do people take flight? Consciously or unconsciously people try to escape because they are not able, or not willing, to face reality. Most likely, they have learned in early life that there are successful ways of escaping the unpleasant. Parents have allowed them to use such methods, or have not taught them to develop other methods of facing reality; this carries on into later life and develops into a pattern of living.

But taking the way of retreat indicates a weakness in a person's character. It is dangerous to develop such a tendency, for ultimately there are conflicts that we are not able to escape. Often the way of escape is cut off for us, and then we find we do not know how to face reality any more.

A person whom I see occasionally had this experience. She lived a rather sheltered life as a child. Then she married a husband who was over-protective, so that she had to face very few conflicts without his support. But the Lord took him from her through death.

Now she has to face all the realities of life alone, and she has never been able to develop sufficient resources to cope with them.

NEEDED CONFLICT

There are choices that you cannot avoid making. You must choose between right and wrong, between good and evil. To try to escape this conflict is folly, for it leads to spiritual bankruptcy. We live in a world of opposites; we face love and hate, war and peace, living and dying, heaven and hell. There is nothing we can do about changing this situation, but we can do something about our own attitudes in such a world.

Conflicts are a means for spiritual growth, growth in character. If you read the biographies of the great men and women of the world, you will note that most of them were people who were able to turn their handicaps into positive assets, to turn their struggles into means of growth. The capacity to find satisfaction within depends upon our ability to accept life's struggles in a practical and realistic way.

The Bible gives us a wonderful truth in Psalm 46 and in other similar passages. "God is our Refuge and our Strength." When you must take flight, when the battle is too hot and conflict too great, God is our Refuge to whom we must go. He is the one to whom we take flight.

But He is also our *Strength* when we face the battles of life. He gives us the strength to fight, the strength to move towards victory. So whether the way of escape must be one of flight, or one of fight—keep your eye on HIM.

44. Learn to Conquer Worry

In a recent study made by the University of Michigan Survey Research Center some rather surprising facts were uncovered about mental health. The survey was based on 2,460 interviews with people who formed an average cross-section of American life.

It was discovered that the vast majority of these people admitted that they did worry, some more than others. Some of the major reasons for unhappiness and worry were finances, inadequate housing and job tensions. Too much debt seemed to be one of the predominant problems in the emotional life of many people.

CAUSE FOR WORRY

Only 17 per cent said that they found real happiness in marriage, and only 14 per cent found happiness in their work. But only 4 per cent were worried about world tensions and the threat of war.

I am sure that such statistics will be substantiated by the average pastor as he thinks of his church. Any counselor who deals with a number of people will find that these facts are true. Generally, the chief source of worry and unhappiness is the little things of everyday living. Many of our worries center in material things. Sometimes these are small things, sometimes larger difficulties; sometimes they are real, and then again they are imagined. But worry is usually concerned with the tangible things of everyday life.

In a way this is a bit surprising. You would think that people would be more worried about the big things of life. After all, we are living in times that seem threatening and may be even more threatening for our children in years to come. Much of the material security upon which people once rested has been brushed aside in recent years.

But the basic worries of people do not change very much. The things we worry about are the things our fathers and mothers worried about, and they are also the things that Jesus warned about in His day. Even then these worries were common.

But according to this University of Michigan study the predominant anxiety that eats away at the vitality of American life is based upon a materialistic view of life. It is anxiety over eating and drinking and health and shelter and the work we do from day to day. This indicates what most people think about most of the time and what is uppermost in the mind and heart of man.

WHAT DO THEY DO ABOUT IT?

The survey also showed that most people do nothing about the problems they face. They just go on fretting and worrying and hoping that sooner or later their problems will pass away. They are never quite happy, although they do have moments when they forget their concerns. They often live with a heavy heart, but do little about it.

Some did mention talking over their problems with spouse or other relative who might be able to help them. A large number of them read books and magazines that give advice on better mental health. This would account for the ever-increasing number of books on the subject. Books on how to overcome worry and fear often become best sellers.

16 per cent of the people surveyed found help in prayer, and almost a third of the number felt that it did help to pray when they faced a real crisis. This is a wholesome sign, although the percentage is a bit discouraging.

Of those who went to seek help from others, especially in more serious personal problems, 42 per cent turn to ministers, 29 per cent to the family doctor and 18 per cent to psychiatrists, psychologists and industrial counselors.

About one third of the 2500 people surveyed reported that they had been near the brink of a nervous breakdown at some point in life, due to severe losses and serious job tensions.

AN ANTIDOTE FOR WORRY

There should be one great difference, however, between Christians and non-Christians. We face the same problems, but we have learned to handle them in a different way. If we really believe that our Christian faith reaches down into every part of life, if we accept the fact that God in His providence rules all things in life, should we then not be able to cast aside our worries when they arise, and learn to cling to the God who controls even the storms of life?

For our mental health, and the mental health of our families, it is most important that we find an antidote for worry, a prescription for our anxiety, a way of escape from our tensions. For worry can undermine a person's health. The word "worry" literally means "to divide." Worry divides the mind between worthwhile interests and damaging thoughts.

Besides this, worry is very contagious. A worry-wart in the family can cause the whole family to be upset, especially if the worrier is a parent. People seldom worry alone; they tell others about their concern and others worry with them.

Worry is useless. Jesus makes this plain when he says, "Which of you by being anxious can add one cubit to the measure of his stature?" Worry never did anyone any good, it never solved a single problem, it never helped a person to win a battle. It always divides the person.

How do we overcome worry? Some will say, by prayer and faith. This is true. But we must be a bit careful here. I know a lot of people who also pray worrisome prayers. Their prayers are burdened with concerns, and somehow these prayers do not help to lift the load.

OUR VIEW OF LIFE

What is rather required is taking a different attitude towards life. For worry speaks of a fretful, feverish way of looking at life with its problems. As Christians we need not take a light-hearted or frivolous approach to life, but we should try to take a more confident and secure attitude — one that is not upset by every obstacle and difficulty, but that can ride serenely on over the rough spots.

We can learn to smile at the difficulties and overcome the frustrations of life when we are ready to leave all in the hands of a sovereign and all-wise God. Take life seriously, but do not take yourself so seriously!

For the real victory over worry is the victory over ourselves — a victory that we will learn only at the feet of one who never worried even though he was heavily burdened. He walked among the lilies of the field and said, "If therefore God so clothe the grass of the field, will he not much more clothe you, o ye of little faith?" He said, "Look at the birds of the air; they neither sow nor reap, nor gather into barns, yet your heavenly father feedeth them. Are you not of more value than they?"

45. Being Driven by the Clock

When our schools open their doors for the fall season, it brings a change in the pattern of our home life. Children will no longer be around the home, but each marches off in the morning to his or her place of learning. Life moves on a more regular schedule.

In the summer months the affairs of the family can be a little less structured, a bit more casual. But then, we must live by the clock. Each morning and each noon, there is the rush to get off to school before the tardy bell rings.

CLOCK WATCHING

Most of us do a lot of clock watching. It begins in the early morning when, with sleepy eyes, we turn off the alarm clock. The kitchen clock drives us to gulp down our breakfast rather hurriedly and then we rush off to punch the time clock at our place of work.

This goes on throughout the day, until the clock tells us that it is time to go to bed. Clocks are hung in conspicuous places so that we can readily check the time of the day. Even in churches the clock is hung so that the ministers can preach according to the allotted time.

There is something inescapable about this. We all have our schedules to meet, we must be at certain places at a certain time. This is good too, for it brings a certain regularity to life.

DANGERS

But it also has its dangers. Some people are driven by the hands of the clock. Mothers in the home will tell of the fact that they carry out all their work according to a fixed time schedule. They determine that the dishes should be finished by a certain time, another set time is provided for dusting, or washing the clothes. They hurry along to get things done within that set time.

In this way time becomes the master, and we become the slaves to those cruel hands that move relentlessly on. The result is that they feel pressured by time. They get that hurried feeling, and it creates tensions.

WORKING BY A SCHEDULE

It is a good thing to work by a schedule. Most of us do not schedule our time as well as we might. We could accomplish better work, more consistent work, if we had a good schedule. But then it is important to remember that such a schedule is a tool, not an end in itself.

For even a schedule can become a cruel taskmaster, if we allow it to dominate our lives. It is not healthy to work under such a strain. Such means of regulating our life must always be flexible enough to allow for change.

DRUDGERY

Constantly being driven by the passing of time can make our work seem like drudgery. In such a state of mind, it is not the joy of doing that work that grips us, but the satisfaction of saying, "I have finished it." I pity the man who must find satisfaction in that way.

Life in a mental hospital can teach us a few lessons about the value of time. The hours and days in such a setting move along slowly. For the great value of passing time is not just in the hours that we count by the clock, but what we have put into those hours, and how we have spent these hours.

Many people will tell us that they broke down due to overwork. This is usually not the case. It is not the amount of work that was done or required, it was the way that work was done. When people go about their tasks in a fretful feverish way, constantly being driven by the hands of the clock, or the numbers of the calendar, they break under the strain. This is an attitude which should be avoided at all cost.

JESUS' WAY OF WORKING

I often marvel at the calm leisureliness in which our Lord went about his work. He was busy, but never rushed. He had time to do his work, but also to note the birds of the heavens, the flowers of the field and the children playing in the market place. He also found time to commune with his heavenly Father.

I think we can learn a lesson from him, also in the use of our time. For time may not become our master to drive us, but it is to be the tool that we use to accomplish our work. It is like the room in which we perform life's task.

When you catch yourself being driven by the clock, it is well to sit down and consider why you are rushing so. God gives us enough time in which to do the work He requires of us. He expects us to use that time in the most efficient way. He expects no more.

46. The Search for Security

People are always trying to find a fitting label for the age in which we live. One that is frequently heard and read is that this is an age of anxiety and insecurity. We need not look far to realize the truth of this description. Bill Mauldin, the cartoonist, in one of his picture interpretations calls this a "scared-rabbit" generation. This does seem to describe the mad and restless quest for security.

But many feel that we have every right to feel insecure in a time like this. Many of the securities, which men trusted, have been taken away from us. The dollar today is worth only fifty cents. The powerful weapons that once gave us such a sense of complacency have been dangerously duplicated by other nations. Our leaders often seem to be lost in the mess of international relationships. Today guided missiles are in the hands of misguided men. We read and listen each day wondering what new crisis will be reported.

It is a bit paradoxical that it should be so. This is also an era in which we have been promised great social security. We have protection for old age, for illness and for unemployment. But we tend to lack a firm trust even in these promised securities. The cause for our feelings of insecurity is not in these external things, but in man himself who has lost his personal sense of security. In this, our age is not so different from previous generations, for this weakness is as old as sin, and springs even from the gates of Eden.

INSECURE FEELINGS

People have met this feeling of insecurity in various ways. Many find refuge in tranquilizers and sleeping pills, which are readily available today. Others find questionable relief in the use of alcohol. Such people are hiding their heads in the sand, and wake up the next day even more troubled than the day before.

Others strike out in hostile attitudes towards others, for they lose their sense of calm reasoning. In ugly suspicions they strike out at all those who dare to be different. It is always fashionable to blame the government, to condemn the present social order, or even the lack of religion and the inadequacies of the church and its leaders. It relieves many pent-up emotions to blame the Communists and the Russians.

There are segments of the church that dream of the millenniums

137

to come, when all the jarring elements will be no more, and men can be secure, perfectly secure.

But, in the meantime, men move on in the search for security, and the next generation is nurtured in an atmosphere that is unhealthy — mentally, emotionally and spiritually. For, the basic insecurity lies in us. And when we are nurtured in such an atmosphere, where will the next generation stand? It is most uncomfortable to live in a "scared-rabbit" generation.

FACING THE FACTS

The primary rule in solving any problem is to face the facts squarely. We are being subjected to much propaganda. In recent years many books and articles have appeared which seem to have a purpose of frightening people into an acceptance of how bad the situation really is. We would get the impression that our own country is about ready to disintegrate, while the Communist nations are forever gaining in strength. I dare say there is some truth in all these documents, but we are called upon to carefully sift the evidence as it is given to us.

Facing the facts means that we look at the facts in a calm and unemotional way. We must view them in the calm light of reason and common sense. It is easy to whip up a crowd to frenzy, anxiety, or even hate. But a secure person is one who views the facts and then calculates his conclusions.

This is something we must learn in every problem we have in life, whether it is a quarrel with one's wife, a discussion with one's neighbor, or a question of bomb shelters. This is something we must teach our children, for they too must learn to solve their questions above the sphere of the emotions.

CLING TO BASIC VALUES

The approach we take to the facts that surround us depends upon our sense of values. The man whose ultimate values rest in the material world will naturally feel insecure when the stock markets decline and depressions loom on the horizon. He has been building on sinking sand.

Even when one's sense of values rests upon the ultimate goodness of man, or the accomplishments of technology and science, the basis for security is too flimsy. Such a person may feel secure, but his securities will vanish at the portals of eternity.

The Psalmist lived in a more quiet time, in a world that moved at a slower pace. But he also felt the ravaging results of war, he felt the pinch of poverty, he also knew of the threatening power of

Egypt, Babylon, and Syria. But in the midst of all this his faith was secure, for he could say, "The Lord is my shepherd, I shall not want." And when there were great crises, he was not a "scared rabbit," he did not just whistle in the dark to keep up courage. There might be wars, he could be carried off as a captive slave, he might even lose his life. But he could say, "I will fear no evil; for thou art with me."

The restless search for security finds its goal when the soul finds security in the inescapable God. It is when the guilty one finds refuge in a gracious Savior that he finds security for this life and the next.

This is a security that is born "beside the still waters."

DEVELOPING A SENSE OF VALUES

. . . .Let every man take heed how he buildeth. . . .
for other foundation can no man lay then that which is
laid, which is Jesus Christ.

Now if any man build on this foundation gold, silver,
precious stones, wood, hay, stubble;
every man's work shall be made manifest;

for the day shall declare it,
because it shall be revealed by fire;
and the fire shall try every man's work
of what sort it is.

— St. Paul, in I Corinthians 3:11-13

47. Aimless Living

"The great sickness of our age is aimlessness, boredom and lack of meaning and purpose in living. We can be enthralled by the space age, but almost willfully try to avoid learning how to understand and control ourselves."

This diagnosis of the ills of our generation was given by Dr. Dana L. Farnsworth at a recent meeting of the American Medical Association. Dr. Farnsworth is director of health services at Harvard University and staff physician at Massachusetts General Hospital in Boston.

The press release of his address quoted him further as saying, "Medicine has made enormous strides in alleviating pain and prolonging life, now an expanded task for doctors is to give meaning to life." I suppose one could quarrel with the doctor about his treatment of the illness, but few of us would question his diagnosis.

LACK OF ADEQUATE GOALS

Much of the prevailing restlessness and tension of society today is born out of sheer aimlessness. There are many who lack an adequate purpose for living. They take a joy-rider's attitude towards the pilgrimage of life for they are indifferent both as to direction and destination. They drift along with the tide of time and so make little progress.

There seem to be an ever increasing number of young people who do not know what their life's vocation is to be. Many are already enrolled in college who have not chosen a life's work. This is often blamed upon the uncertainty of the times, and the fact that they may have to interrupt their training by a period of service in the armed forces. But it is actually a symptom of the lack of purpose which is so prevalent today.

Some do have a driving goal, but it is one that is unworthy of the Christian. Wealth, fame and power beckon some. Sensual gratification is a lure for others. But if the highest goal of any man is centered in something material it cannot give lasting satisfaction, even though he should reach the goal. It can give fleeting satisfaction to keep up with the Joneses, but it is not an adequate goal to give meaning to living.

INTEGRATION OF RESOURCES

The failure to have worthwhile objectives leads to a disintegration of the resources of the individual. He is like the Knight who put on his armor, mounted his horse, and drove off in all directions. The basic meaning of the word "anxiety" is to be torn asunder by various inner conflicts.

No one perhaps ever achieves a completely integrated personality. There will always be conflicts, tensions between the secular and the spiritual, the flesh and the spirit. There will be struggles between the standards and values of the social group and the demands of a soul wholly committed to Christ. But the measure of our maturity is the measure of our inner integration. Complete disintegration of the resources of personality means a very serious kind of mental illness.

How then do we achieve consistency and inner unity? This can only be accomplished by establishing a dominant purpose in life. When our whole life is directed towards one, all-embracing goal, the scattered forces of the person will be unified to accomplish that purpose.

In most democratic nations there are many factions. One political party quarrels with another, one economic block struggles with another, one race or color clashes with another. When you read the news you would feel that such a country is at the point of falling apart. But if tomorrow this same nation is attacked by an enemy from without, all the vast resources of that nation will stand shoulder to shoulder to defend that which it represents.

This is also true in the life of a person. I know of a good many people who suffered from conflicts, tensions and anxieties. Upon the advice of a psychiatrist or pastor they have interested themselves in some worth-while project, or some kingdom enterprise. The result was that life had new meaning for them. They had a purpose and a goal, and their life moved into more constructive channels. Many volunteer workers in hospitals, children's homes, and similar institutions have gained great rewards for their own mental health.

THE HIGHEST GOAL

But the question is: What are the goals we should be seeking? To what purposes should we give our lives? What should be the aim of all our striving in these few years God gives us?

Jesus has given us the answer in the gospel, "Seek ye first the Kingdom of God and His righteousness." It is also stated in the commands, "Thou shalt love God above all . . . and thy neighbor as thyself." This must become the dominating purpose. No lower goal will ever do.

No better illustration of this can be found than our Lord himself. This was his purpose in all that He did. That is why his personality was unified and integrated in a perfect way.

If you gain the goal towards which you are striving today, where will you be when you reach life's eventide?

48. Our Sense of Values

One of the primary things in a healthy mental life for ourselves and our children is to develop a worthwhile sense of values. We must ask ourselves at times, "What are the things that I value most in life?" In the lives of all of us there are some things we consider to be most important, other things we consider to be of lesser importance, and some things we consider to be of least value to us.

MATERIAL VALUES

In our age, wealth is often considered to be of greatest value. Those who take this attitude suppose that making money and obtaining the things that money can buy are a worthwhile objective for living. Many use the time and energy of fifty or sixty years in quest of money. For some, money becomes the chief aim of living; every effort is spent in its pursuit, and often other values are sacrificed to achieve it.

The obtaining of various forms of selfish amusement and happiness is often set up as the greatest value in life. Those who have this attitude seek to please themselves in a personal way, often even at the expense of others. Usually, the more they seek this kind of ephemeral joy, the more they lose the higher and deeper joys of life.

Dr. Temple, the Archbishop of Canterbury during the World War II years, states in one of his addresses, "The world we live in is like a shop window in which some mischievous person has shifted all the price labels, so that the cheap things have high-priced labels and the really precious things are priced cheaply." Then he added, "We have let ourselves be taken in."

IMPORTANCE

Why is a sense of values so important? It is the barometer that indicates what we really are in the depths of our being. It shows the kind of stuff of which we are made and reveals the motivation of our actions and the goals towards which we move.

One way in which we frequently express our sense of values is in the words "It's worth it." We make a sacrifice for something, or we suffer for it, but we say "It was really worth it."

We often indicate our sense of values in different ways. For we show what we consider to be worthwhile to us in the way we live. The man who stays in bed on Sunday morning shows that he is putting a higher value on his physical comfort than on self-discipline and worship, even though he may not admit to this fact verbally.

A man may say, "I believe the truth of the Bible." But if he seldom reads his Bible, he shows that he does not value his Bible so highly.

How then can we judge our sense of values? A real value remains even if all other things are taken from us—that which no circum-stances in life can debase, that which gives an inner satisfaction which we can get in no other way.

VALUES AND MENTAL HEALTH

But what has all this to say about our mental health? I feel strongly that the person who debases his sense of values does violence to the dignity of his own soul. He violates the very purpose for which he was made, and he casts aside the objectives for which he was redeemed.

Man is a spiritual being, but he has a body. This body with all its marvelous elements was given him to give expression to his spiritual and mental self. When man turns about and makes the physical his ultimate goal, he loses his dignity as God's image-bearer and does violence to his own nature.

This leads to basic conflicts, conflicts between man as he knows he ought to be and as he knows he is. Paul describes this as the struggle between the flesh and the spirit. This is basically a struggle in man's inner self.

The only way out of this struggle is with God's help to set our values high, and then to strive to make our lives conform to these loftier goals of living.

I can think of no better way to resolve this struggle than to be reminded often of who we are and of the great price that has been paid for our redemption, and of our ultimate destiny.

In so doing we raise our sense of values to conform with Christian ideals, and we set all the energies of our minds and emotions into motion to reach these values as the really worthwhile goals of all living.

One day we shall be able to look back upon the battles, the sacrifices, even the fierce fightings in our inner selves and say, "It was really worth it."

49. Our Needs and Our Wants

A well-known confection has had as its slogan for many years, "The more you eat, the more you want." I am not so sure that the slogan is true. It is not as far as I am concerned. But I do know that it is true as far as success is concerned.

Success is a magic word in American life that describes the desires of many. But when you try to define the term, you find that it is measured often in terms of material values. The advertisements on radio and TV or in magazines hold out before us the things that make a man successful. He has a better car, a larger home and a more remunerative job.

Now, there is nothing wrong with the desire to improve our standard of living. But when this striving becomes so strong that it can never reach a point of satisfaction then it is dangerous and unhealthy.

Our needs can always be satisfied, but how about our wants?

DREAMING OF SUCCESS

It is normal for a child to have day-dreams of becoming someone of importance, or of having something he now misses. Every boy dreams of owning a sleek car, and every girl wants to marry the young man of her ideals.

But when we mature, those dreams can get out of hand if we do not limit them. For dreams of success lead to striving for more, no matter how much we have. Striving after success has this slogan, "The more you strive, the more you want. The more you want, the more you strive." This becomes a vicious cycle that is hard to break.

It has happened often that people gained a measure of success in a material way. They have a good income, a better than average home, and all the gracious living that goes with it. But when this has been attained they are unhappy because there are others who have a nicer home or a larger income.

They forget to enjoy what they have because their wants grow with every acquisition in life. They seek happiness, not in what they have at present, but in what they hope to have in the future.

REALITY—A SOURCE OF HAPPINESS

Only present reality can give genuine satisfaction. The desires and wants are for the future. Many successful people break down mentally and emotionally because they have forgotten that there will always be differences between people. It is always going to be true that there are some others who have more than we do.

Success is relative. It is hard to measure it. But we make a tragic mistake when we measure it in terms of material things. It needs also the measuring rod of character, of personal satisfaction and of spiritual returns.

It is a tragic sense of values that measures a man in terms of what he has rather than in terms of what he is.

LIMITING OUR DESIRES

No person may ever allow his desires to get out of control. It is one of the surest roads to mental breakdown. All our desires must have bounds, also the desire for success.

A young man had been given a very fine promotion. His salary had doubled and he could now afford many of the things he always wanted. But the strain of his new position made him unhappy and depressed. He could not handle it.

Actually he was emotionally unfit for the new position. He felt that he had failed and he asked to be returned to his old job. He was a person who had to limit his desires because of his own emotional needs.

There are many like him. You often meet them in mental hospitals. They should have limited their wants.

SPIRITUAL LIMITATIONS

There are some who gain a measure of success and it leads to tragic results in their spiritual life. While attaining social and material gains, they suffer spiritual loss. Here too, a wise man will limit his desires according to his spiritual capacities. There can be little satisfaction in "gaining the world and losing our souls."

Success alone does not bring joy, and striving for it can lead to greater unhappiness. This is just as true for those who never attain success, but who always wish for it, as for those who do attain it.

Many psychiatrists believe that ceaseless striving for more, with all its accompanying emotional stress, is one of the most common causes of mental distress.

For most Americans "our needs can always be met, but our wants can never be satisfied." When we consider our present blessings we have received from God, it would be far wiser and emotionally healthier to count our blessings than to be concerned about our unfulfilled dreams and desires.

50. Making Decisions

Life requires of all of us an unending series of decisions. We are constantly making choices between various alternatives. Some are of minor importance, other decisions are of far-reaching importance in our lives. Often we must decide between an either-or proposition, sometimes there are various alternatives, and then again it may be a matter of whether we shall make a decision or not. In every choice we give evidence to the strength of character and will we have.

Vacillation is a problem for many. They are like the people of whom the apostle James writes, "He that wavereth is like the waves of the sea." An insecure person finds himself constantly on the fence wondering whether he should go this way or that. In fact most of us have certain areas of life in which we find it difficult to make definite choices. When this reaches into various areas of life it can be very troublesome, and may undermine efficiency and mental health.

A teen-age girl may have a hard time deciding which dress or outfit she is going to wear for the day at school. She will try on two or three different ones and then feels dissatisfied throughout the day because she has picked the wrong one. I know of ministers who have this problem in choosing a text for the sermon for the coming Sunday. They may pick and choose several times, and finally they must select something because the materials must be ready for the church bulletin.

Often this difficulty in making choices has its roots in early life. Some parents insist on making all the decisions for their children. This is fine when they are very young, but early in life children should learn to make simple choices. As the years go on they must be taught to make up their own minds, to make wise choices, but to make them independently. This is part of the growth and development of character, for there are choices parents cannot make for their children.

Others lack self-confidence and hence have a feeling of insecurity in the choices of life. Some feel that they must first consult others.

This can develop to such a point where the person is unable to do constructive work. Still others do not want to make decisions. Choosing is often painful, and it is so much easier just to sit back and let nature take its course.

But in our present society a measure of decisiveness is important. If we are to be contributing members of society, of the family, or of the church, this expression of the will must become evident. In fact, you cannot even drive your car without making many choices.

FAR-REACHING DECISIONS

Some of life's choices are major ones. The choice of a partner for life is one of these. When a young man chooses a young lady from among all the members of the fairer sex, he is making a choice for life. It is a choice that can never be taken lightly. When once the sacred vows have been spoken it is "till death do us part." Small wonder that such a decision has frightened many a timid soul.

The choice of a vocation also falls in this area. It becomes a matter of selecting in the vast market-place of life. This seems to be more difficult today than in former years.

In such choices we may not decide with our heart only, but also with our head. We must weigh the evidence carefully, and then select as best we can. This should never be done in haste and always in a prayerful spirit.

BASIC REQUIREMENTS

To make wise decisions we need a dependable standard of judgment. There must be a basic sense of values. If our standards are those of self-interest, material gain, or simply picking the easiest way out, they fall far below the ideals of the Christian life. Only worthy, God-glorifying and spiritual goals should guide us.

Decisions take courage. That is why in our day there are many who do not make decisions. It's so much more pleasant to be "tolerant" and "open-minded." Such shallow views of living cannot satisfy a thinking man. There are times when we must stand firm and say, "I can do no otherwise, so help me God." This requires all the powers of a strong will.

LIFE'S GREATEST DECISION

Basically then, all our choices in life must be colored by the answer we give to the great choice that all men must make, "Choose ye this day whom ye will serve." This is the fork of the road to which all must come. And when we choose the road that leads God-ward and heavenward we have set a standard of judgment by which all life's decisions will be measured.

How marvelous then that this is not just the choice of a road, but a decision to follow a Person who still says, "I am the way."

51. The Frustrated Perfectionist

One of the distinguishing marks of a rug made by the American Indians is that there is always a defect in its design. These people believe that only their gods can, and should, be perfect. A perfectly symmetrical and flawless rug would seem to them to be an offense to the gods. They make "mistakes" on purpose, to show that they are human.

There are many people who could learn a lesson from these Indians. Those of us who think we must achieve perfection in everything we do are setting our standards too high for human attainment. Such people tend to break down because they torment themselves with so strict a way of living that it becomes absurd and exaggerated.

Perfectionism reveals itself in many ways: in the work we do, in running an office, in our personal appearance, in our love life, and in our social relationships. When it takes hold of us, perfectionism constitutes a major cause of unrest and unhappiness.

THESE "PERFECT" PEOPLE

After all, there is no such thing as a perfect person, and it is sheer waste of energy to try to be one. Perfection, in whatever field, is unattainable. It is a goal always beyond our grasp.

Some home-makers strive for perfection in their work. In time they become regular dirt-chasers. They spend their time scrubbing, polishing, and dusting, and, as most of you know, they never reach a point where there is no dust or dirt left. When you visit such a home you feel like taking your shoes off at the door and sitting on the edge of the chair, for fear you might muss up the doilies. This may make a beautiful house, but it makes a terrible home.

Girls in their late teens often have a perfectionist ideal about love and marriage. They are looking for a man without faults. Fortunately, as time passes, and romance passes them by, they change their philosophy of love. They find out that there is no such person as a perfect man, and that the ideal husband is a human one.

Some girls spend hours before a mirror, primping and fussing. When they leave, every hair must be in place and every eyelash properly spaced. Their clothing must be perfectly matched. Such people are a great support for beauty-parlors. By overly meticulous grooming they try to compensate for inadequacies in other areas.

It is well to discover that people do not like us because of our perfection. They accept us because we are human, and to be human is to have faults.

Men like to feel that they can be of help to their wives, to teach them to correct certain faults. A wife likes to have a husband whom she feels she can improve and inspire. It gives her a feeling of being needed and useful.

We frequently counsel people who have feelings of spiritual inadequacy. Women, in certain stages in life, have feelings that they are not good Christians. Their spiritual life has not developed as it should. Some will feel unworthy to partake of communion, because they are not good enough. They will even begin to wonder whether they are Christians.

I have frequently asked such strugglers, "What kind of housekeeper are you? Can you stand to see a little dust on the living-room table?" Almost inevitably they will confess that they are overly meticulous homemakers.

Being an exaggeratedly clean housekeeper is seemingly unrelated to a person's spiritual and emotional life. But this is not the case. If we have perfectionist standards in one area, we are bound to carry them over into other areas of life. Those who torment themselves by setting unattainable standards in material things will also torment themselves in the same way with spiritual things.

THE HAPPY MEDIUM

We may as well resign ourselves to the fact that there will always be faults in everything we do. Each morning anew we will have to resolve to conquer our errors and sins, and each evening we will have new sins to confess. When we do so, we need not torment ourselves or consider ourselves to be failures; we are merely being human.

The goal of Scripture is clearly stated, "Be ye perfect." But our Lord, knowing our human weaknesses, teaches us to pray each day, "Forgive us our debts." There are goals that we shall not reach on the road of sanctification here below. But we shall reach them one day in heaven, made perfect through glorification.

TOWARDS
EMOTIONAL AND SPIRITUAL MATURITY

For we know in part, and we prophesy in part.
But when that which is perfect is come,
then that which is in part shall be done away.
When I was a child, I spake as a child,
I understood as a child,
I thought as a child;
But when I became a man, I put away childish things.
For now we see through a glass, darkly;
but then face to face;
now I know in part; but then shall I know even as also
*   I am known.*
And now abideth faith, hope, love, these three;
But the greatest of these is love.

— St. Paul, in I Corinthians 13

52. The Perils of Pessimism

There are people who look at everything from the dark side. They search out the shadows and set their hearts on walking in them. Wherever they go they leave behind a little touch of gloom. They take literally the words of Solomon when he says, "Sorrow is better than laughter." They sing life's song in a minor key.

We usually do not seek out the company of those that move through life with a frown instead of a smile, for they tend to make life difficult for themselves and for others. They make sorrow more difficult to bear, because they exaggerate it. The battle of life seems more severe when they fight it. The whole effect of their lives is one of gloom.

A GLOOMY OUTLOOK

I dare say, some people are happiest when they are sad. They enjoy it when they can find something unpleasant to talk about. They even consider themselves benefactors of their fellow men, because they are watchmen on the walls, pointing out life's dangers. But, actually, they are a peril, both to themselves and to others.

Notice some of the burdens that depress them. The weather is quite a favorite topic, because it is usually too hot or too cold. The spreader of gloom is sure that the excessive rain will spoil the crop. But if it does not rain, there is the solemn prediction that the crop is going to fail. The weather is never quite right, because it bothers either his asthma or his rheumatism.

The situation in the world is also a favorite burden. The world is on its way to ruin, for it will not be long before the Communists take over and deprive us of what is left of our civilization. When economic conditions are good, there is danger of inflation; when they are poor, we will surely have a depression. Crime and delinquency are on the increase, and more and more people are losing their minds or dying of cancer.

Another burden that gives them food for gloomy thoughts and words is the sad condition of the church. The prophets of gloom speak of the sad decline of spiritual life and of the lack of real interest in the kingdom. They feel that things were much better in a former generation, for today the preaching is less profound, and we have introduced too many new things. We are reminded that all innovations are not improvements.

No wonder that the pessimist is burdened with a heavy load.

157

With a heart full of worry and an eye that sees only the dark shadows, he stumbles through the twilight zone of today into an even darker tomorrow.

WHAT IS WRONG?

What is wrong with such people? For we all realize that life cannot be that gloomy. I do not believe that a pessimistic outlook is only a lack of faith, for many of these pessimists are Christians—gloomy Christians, but sincere. I would feel, rather, that this outlook is an expression of an unwholesome emotional outlook on life. There are people that find more satisfaction in sorrow than in joy, in tears than in laughter. There are many who find more delight in being negative than in being positive.

Often you can already see this in children and young people. Some people begin to worry early in life, and they carry a worrying attitude with them along the whole journey of life. It is hard to change an emotional outlook upon life. But it can be done.

CHANGE OF VIEW

It is possible for a pessimist to become an optimist, but only when he learns to take a different view of life. Our viewpoint depends on the color of the lenses through which we see and interpret events. As Christians, we must learn to discard the dark-colored glasses, for there are great perils in pessimism.

We can do great damage to those about us by being disciples of gloom. For one thing, we greatly impair our Christian witness. We give the impression that religion is a gloomy thing. Actually, if there is anyone in this world who has a right to laugh, it is the Christian. For the laughter of the world is but hollow mockery.

I am not suggesting a Pollyanna view of life. We need to face life realistically and practically. But at the same time, we know that He who holds the world in his hand will make all things work out for good. Even the song that begins in a minor key ends with the song of hope.

53. How Old Are You?

This is just a simple question, one that we often ask and often answer. Some of the members of the fairer sex are supposed to have a reputation for hiding the real answer to the question. But all of us are a bit reluctant to tell our true age. For age is measured in several different ways. It all depends upon our approach to the question.

I would like to ask it in four different ways, and I believe that, if we are honest with ourselves, we will have to give four different answers.

YOUR CHRONOLOGICAL AGE

We can measure our age by the calendar. There are times when we have to obtain our birth certificate in order to prove without question that we are to be considered an adult.

There is however a vast difference in standards of measuring our chronological age. If you were a baseball player you would be considered to be old at thirty-five—forty. There are many factories reluctant to engage a man after he has reached the half century mark. Often churches consider a minister who is over fifty to be "one of our older men." They are interested in someone younger. There may be good reasons for this way of thinking, but basically, it is not the best standard of judgment.

The calendar method of judging age is a very one-sided one. Some people are older at forty-five than others are at sixty. There are other factors that should be taken into consideration.

YOUR PHYSIOLOGICAL AGE

You can also measure your age by the condition of your arteries, or your heart. How old are you physically? There is a great diversity here among people. Our doctors frequently write into a patient report, "this person appears much older than her actual age."

Medical science has done much to stretch out this aspect of the aging process. We have not yet found the "fountain of youth" or the "elixir of life." We are all still being consumed by the "little bites of death." But modern science has done much to enable men to stretch out the physical span of life.

Good rules of healthful living, prompt and efficient medical attention can do much to preserve our physiological age. We may not needlessly throw away some of the years of life.

YOUR PSYCHOLOGICAL AGE

The cry of man has often been, "backwards, turn backwards, O time in your flight." As far as the calendar age is concerned this cry is all in vain. As far as our physiological age is concerned we can do a little. But as far as our psychological age is concerned we can do much. For this is a matter of our attitudes, our mental and emotional state.

Sometimes children of ten are little grandmothers, others at sixteen are still emotionally babies. There are teen-agers who have been drinking so deeply at the experiences of life that they are old far beyond their years. Some people are chronologically in the age of bi-focals but actually are still in the lollipop stage.

In other words, we must strive to develop attitudes, emotions and desires which equip us to face the years of life in which we find ourselves. We should not try to be older than our age, nor should our behavior be that of one younger than our years.

YOUR SPIRITUAL AGE

We do not expect a nine old to have the same spiritual feelings and attitudes that we would find in a person of forty. Our spiritual growth should gradually move on toward maturity and as the years go on it should ripen with age. This takes a lifelong struggle, in prayer, in faith and consecration.

Sad to say, this is not always the case. Our spiritual life is often closely intertwined with our emotional and psychological development. In fact, I have noted that people who are emotionally immature are usually also spiritually immature.

This would then mean that we must all work for a balanced development. Our spiritual growth should keep up with our chronological age. This life may not begin at forty or at fifty. It should be part of us every step of the way.

For when the clock strikes for us at threescore and ten, there is no greater satisfaction and joy than to be able to look back upon a life that has been spent from earliest dawn to life's sunset in the fellowship of our Lord.

Yes, it is important to answer the question, "How old are you?"

54. Putting Away Childish Things

We have all heard of the evil of arrested development. Most of us carry over certain childish tendencies into our later years. Many, if not most, of our emotional problems result from the fact that we have not "put away childish things." For often that which is healthy in a child reveals itself to be very unhealthy when carried over into adult life.

A little baby may sometimes be fretful and irritable, but we expect this from one of tender years. But when a big baby acts the same way it becomes impossible to bear. A child is lovely and attractive, but when he fails to grow he becomes a disappointment and a heartache to all around him.

There are some who have never gotten over letting mother bear the brunt of responsibility. They cling to their mother's apron strings. Sometimes mothers encourage this and do their children a real disservice. For when such a person in adult life faces frustration or danger he may not have a mother to turn to, and he feels lost, and retreats to whatever person or thing may seem to give him a substitute for mother. Many find their way to a psychiatrist's office.

Now, I am sure that none of us really want to be immature. Few of us are really aware of the childish things that remain in our personality. We want to be grown-up. But in many ways we do cling to the childish emotions and attitudes.

OUR CHILDISH WAYS

There are those who never get over throwing temper tantrums. We all know persons who will fly into a rage at the slightest provocation. They will even tell you that they have quite a temper, but that steel is of no value without a good temper. Actually, they are childish folk who have never learned the art of self-control. They are a danger to themselves and to others.

Some children have found by experience that it was convenient to be sick. A headache was a good excuse for getting out of some unpleasant task, or to stay home from school. Later in life they still find this a good way of getting out of work, an unpleasant appointment, or some social function. They often are an absentee problem in their factories and account for a good many empty pews in church.

There are others who will sulk and pout like children. They have found that this is a good method of getting their way. Adding a few well-timed tears can also be helpful. Carrying these tendencies over into later life may serve as an effective means of getting their way, but it constitutes a great emotional hazard.

WHAT'S WRONG WITH CHILDISHNESS?

What is wrong with the childish adult? I rather like the interpretation given by Fritz Kunkel in his book, *In Search of Maturity.* In a child there is a strong sense of ego-feeling. He thinks in terms of himself, of his own needs, no matter how inconvenient it may be to the rest of the family. He has not developed to the place where he can think in terms of others. We are all born as egoists. But as we grow emotionally and mentally, as well as physically, we must move away from the "I" attitude to the "we" attitude. This is something that every child must be taught.

This is where we as parents often fail miserably. We find a certain feeling of satisfaction in the dependence of our children upon us, with the result that we are reluctant to have our children develop a feeling of selfhood.

Selfishness must grow into unselfishness. This will always require a struggle, for within us is always the battle between egoism and altruism. It requires a certain amount of growing pains to move from the "I-feeling" toward the "we-feeling." But we have not been placed in this world to remain children, nor to remain childish. We are not here just for self, but also for others.

TOWARDS GREATER SPIRITUAL MATURITY

This infantile hang-over is evident also in the religious life. There are some who never grow beyond the "Now I lay me down to sleep" level of prayer. Their prayers are for self, but seldom for others. Some Christian people have never read an adult religious book. They are content to be just "babes in Christ."

The message of the Christian faith indicates that self-denial is one of the first requirements of entrance into the Kingdom. The cure for childishness is a childlike attitude. There is no school in this world where this can be taught, but you can learn this at the feet of Him who gave Himself, without any reservations, for His own.

55. How Mature Are We?

In the course of our lives we grow up physically and we develop mentally. But none of us reach that point in life that we can say that we are completely grown-up emotionally or spiritually. There are only a few of us who even approximate full maturity. There are often elements of childishness left in us.

We are able to observe men in public life, in government, or in the various professions, who seem to develop a high degree of maturity. But most likely their wives, their maids or their secretaries could tell of childish traits they manifest in their everyday life. Even the most mature will reveal such traits in moments of stress. Nurses tell us that no matter how important a man may be, he will still react just like the rest of men when he is pricked with a hypodermic needle.

It is not a question of whether we are mature or not, but how mature are we? We see some of the tragedies in the lives of those who are mentally retarded, but sometimes the man who is emotionally retarded is far more tragic.

I would like to list *some of the qualities* that make a man mature. It will not be necessary to go into detail because these are qualities evident in everyday living. It is good to ask ourselves these questions to determine how mature we really are.

1. *Do we find joy in giving as well as receiving?*

A child wants to receive rather than to give. The immature person also faces life with the attitude, "What am I going to get out of it?" This leads to mean and unworthy emotions.

Maturity brings with it a rich concern for others. It is a growing desire to make the lives of our fellows more pleasant and enjoyable. One of the marks of maturity is, "It is more blessed to give than to receive."

2. *Can we form permanent loyalties?*

One day the little girl will walk arm in arm with her friend and say, "We are pals." Tomorrow she will say, "I'm not talking to her, I hate her." Even a child can make friends, but it takes a mature person to make enduring friendships.

Some husbands find contentment in married life only as long as their wives do everything their way. There are wives who love their husbands only if they never cross their path. But the test of mature loyalties comes when cross currents of conflicting desires arise — when it becomes a matter of "give and take."

Other examples of childish interpersonal relationships are seen in the foreman who cannot keep up his relationships with his men, the executive who cannot work satisfactorily with his secretaries, the minister who cannot work effectively with his people for a longer period of time, or the teacher who must have a new school every few years.

3. How well do we face up to competition?

It is hard for a child to learn to play games, especially when it means that he must lose at times. Many adults fall into this same difficulty. Some are overly competitive. They constantly compare themselves with others and carry on a jealous type of rivalry. This generates envy and hostility.

Competition is valuable, it has its place in life. It can be a means to bring out the best in us. But when it becomes too strong, it can bring out the worst in us. When we strive too hard to reach the top, when we feel frustrated when others reach the top before we do, or when we feel threatened when we reach the top first, we are immature in our competition. We have not learned to play the game of life properly.

4. Do we live above the level of hostility and aggressiveness?

Can we live above the level of hate and anger? Some people go through life with a cruel and childish belligerent attitude towards others. Often they are the ones who feel weak and insecure, for only the strong person can afford to be gentle.

Such people are chronic trouble makers. They are experts at stirring up conflicts in the home, in the shop, in the neighborhood and even in the church.

5. Have we learned to be flexible and adaptable.

A child does not react well to new situations. But in adult life we are confronted with changing experiences in life. The mature person learns to be flexible to these changes. He must be able to bend to the varying winds that blow, or he will be broken by them.

We must learn to ride the crest of prosperity, but also the valleys of disappointment. We may not become overly tense and anxious through these varying experiences. Paul tells us that he had learned this secret. He was unspoiled by prosperity and unbroken in adversity for he had learned to be content.

6. Do we have a seasoned faith?

I would not go as far as to say that if a person has no faith he is immature. But in my experience I have observed that if a person is immature in his emotional attitudes, he will also be immature in his spiritual life. For our emotions find expression in faith and trust.

We need a seasoned faith. The faith of childhood is like a fragrant blossom that adorns the tree, in adolescence the petals drop and there is a readiness for a fruitful life, but in spiritual maturity the tree brings forth its fruit in its season. Its root are sunk deep in the stream of God's redemptive work, its sturdy trunk can weather the storms, and the ripened fruits of godliness are seen.

56. Those Twenty Added Years

There are today more people past retirement age than there have ever been before. In the United States there are fifteen million people over sixty-five.

When Caesar ruled in Rome the life expectancy of people was only twenty-seven years. During the days of the Pilgrims it had climbed to thirty-four years. Today the life expectancy of men is sixty-seven and that of women seventy-one. In the last half century twenty years have been added to the expected span of life.

A BLESSING

These twenty years may be counted as a blessing. We all desire to live long, and that is part of a healthy outlook upon life. But added time is in itself not a blessing. Just adding to the succession of days and years may not be an unmixed benefit. It all depends on the content of these years. When these added years become for us a succession of lonely days, filled with morbid reflections, they do not hold much for us. But if they are days of the ripening of the Christian experience, they can be days of comfort for ourselves, our relatives and our friends.

It is true that these added years are often years of fading strength and sometimes chronic illness. The inexorable effects of hardening of the arteries, and other crippling factors, often leave their damaging results in various parts of the body and especially in the brain. This is something over which we have very little control. In such experiences we may but pray that God's grace may be sufficient to bear the thorn in the flesh with dignity and confidence.

MENTAL ATTITUDES

But there are factors over which we do have control and which can make these added years either bitter or sweet; either days of enjoyment, or days when we are a burden to ourselves and our loved ones. I am thinking of our mental attitude towards these latter years. It has been said that when we are older we are what we have been when we were younger, only more so.

This shows so clearly that we need a design of living in earlier days which will accommodate itself also to these latter days. We must prepare ourselves emotionally and mentally for them. We must learn to look upon these added twenty years not as a trying experience that must be faced, but as an adventure to be enjoyed by the grace of God.

There has been much talking and writing about the problems of old age. There are various organizations that deal with the subject of gerontology and geriatrics. They make their contribution. But there is the danger that people think about the closing years of life as years to be dreaded, even to be feared.

MEMORIES

Old age is a time of memories and retrospection. But the content of these memories is not determined in these latter years, but in the earlier years of life. Memories are for some people like travelling again part of the journey of life, journeying through pleasant landscapes with its valleys and mountains. For others, memories are like haunted halls that call up the grim spectres of the past. It is often those whose memories are not too pleasant who find all kinds of mental mechanisms to blot out the past.

It is important to enrich the chambers of the inner man during the earlier days of life with fine cultural and religious furnishings. If we have learned to steep our minds in the legacies of great literature, if we have dipped our souls into the fountains of spiritual and heavenly truths, old age need not be empty and barren.

A PATTERN OF LIFE

Many of us are too busy making a living. We are so filled with the material activities of life that there is scarcely room left for the spiritual. Many find no time for special service in kingdom causes, in spite of the vast opportunities available. Then, when the days of retirement come, we are bored with ourselves, and often become a burden to others.

Set a pattern of living that will accommodate itself to these added years of life. Then these years will not be a burden, but a blessing. For then, "At eventide it will be light." For the Christian the outlook for the future is not "sunset and evening star" but the sunrise of a new and better day.

57. The Fear of Growing Old

As one of our student nurses walked out of our Women's Geriatric Unit the other day she remarked, "I hope I never grow old." It is true that working with people who have lost the full control of their mental powers, due to advancing years, can give a warped view of old age. The student nurse's expression is one which is often heard. To many younger people the thought of old age is frightening. They contrast the limiting factors of old age with their own youthful vigor, and develop a fear of growing old.

We might question whether people really mean it when they say that they would rather die than have an old age in which they are helpless and decrepit. We all love life, even though it may have its pains and aches and sorrows. But there is little in the period of life after seventy that looks appealing to those who are young and healthy.

It is rather hard to tell just when old age begins, but it may be said that one is old after seventy. It is the time of life when the physical energies begin to wane, and when many of the faculties lose their vigor. It is the last mile of the journey of life; and since man was created to live, it is not normal to want to die.

But an inordinate fear of growing old does not speak of a healthy attitude toward life. The fear of growing old invites misery and unhappiness. To let the unpleasant prospect of the future cast a shadow upon life today is utter folly; it betrays an immature approach to life's realities.

WHY WE FEAR OLD AGE

In our generation we have placed a premium on youth. For a man over forty-five years of age it is often difficult to find employment, he is considered too old. This is a strange development in our culture. Never before has the life expectancy of both men and women been so high. During the last twenty-five years the life expectancy has increased by twenty years. But during this same time it has become much more difficult for a man of fifty to find a new job. In an ever increasing number, people are encouraged to retire at sixty-two or sixty-five.

Some time ago a few members of a vacant church were discussing possible candidates for a call to their church. The name of one of my classmates was mentioned among these nominees. One of the group said, "But he would be rather old for our congregation."

It is twenty-eight years ago that our class graduated from the seminary, and this minister is in his early fifties.

There is a rejection of those of more mature years. This implies that, in general, people question whether there is still a useful place in our economy and in the kingdom for those who have a few grey hairs and a number of years of valuable experience.

Age cannot be measured only in terms of years; it must be measured in qualities of character and in terms of the contributions a man can make to society and to the kingdom.

It is small wonder that people dread the feeling of growing old in such a system, if it means that we are then placed on the sidelines or sent out to pasture, because the days of making a contribution are past.

A HEALTHY VIEW

It is important to view each stage in life as a preparation for the next. We must recognize that each changing scene offers opportunities and challenges, as well as disappointments and struggles. The days of youth bring joys and ambitions, but also problems. In the proper solution of these problems lies the secret of successful and constructive years of achievement.

In the years when we are in the strength of life we must make ready for the years when our energies will begin to fail. Each period finds us planning and making ready for the next.

It is this kind of forward look that is needed. None of us need fear the natural process of growing older if we can view life as a training period for greater things beyond. The real test of character is to anticipate the years ahead as years in which life's experiences will deepen. For, even old age offers opportunities that the pressures of more youthful years deny us.

It all depends upon one's mental and spiritual attitude. The man who begins to feel hopeless as soon as he is fitted with his first pair of bi-focals is to be pitied. The man who worries about his grey hair and his slower gait has lost sight of some of the realities of life.

I always love the story of Caleb in the Bible. He was an old man and had had some rugged experiences in his life. But in his old age he asked Joshua for permission to go out to conquer the sons of Anak who lived in the mountain strongholds. At eighty-five he had the courage and perseverance of youth. After he had conquered the stronghold of Hebron he could sit in the door of his mountain home, look out over the valley, and in retrospect he could see his life and say, "I wholly followed the Lord, my God."

58. The Power of Hope

Many books have been written about faith, and also about love, but few have been written about the other members of Paul's familiar triad — hope. It is, however, also one of the great vital powers of our lives.

The dictionary defines hope as "a feeling that what is wanted will happen, a desire accompanied by anticipation and expectation." Karl Menninger submitted the thought that "hope is an awareness of unconscious wishes which, like dreams, tend to come true."

A FRAIL HOPE

In the literature and art of the world the thought of hope has often been minimized. The Greeks considered hope as an evil, for to them it was only an illusion, and a false one at that. The symbol used for hope was that of a frail girl, bending over a lyre. But this instrument which normally has seven strings, had only one string left. Hope is trying to pluck out a tune from this one remaining string.

In everyday language we often use the word hope in the same way. It is often said, "I don't expect it to happen, but I can still have hope." This is not using the word correctly. For hope is "a desire accompanied by anticipation."

There are many who have carried on in life, in spite of great difficulties, because they had a strong hope. We have often met people who have feelings of hopelessness. This is a tragic and devastating feeling. Life seems in vain and the prospect for the future is no brighter. The extreme feelings of hopelessness are found in depressive patients, especially those with suicidal feelings. In my experience, this is the worst suffering that man can endure.

We also know of people who, through the loss of hope, seemed to accelerate the arrival of death. If they lose their hope, they give up the fight for life, and this contributes to the loss of the battle.

Aware that hope is such a vital force in keeping the spark of life aglow, we can readily see that it is also an important power in our lives when we are healthy and in the thick of the battle. A hopeful approach is always a healthy one.

A WORTHWHILE INCENTIVE

Hope affects us in our daily work. When there is no incentive for improvement in the job we fill, we tend to trudge along, finding the routine of life tiresome and boring. But when a man is challenged by his work, he has something that drives him and gives joy to his tasks.

We all need something to draw us, to encourage us to do our best, to goad us to achieve greater heights. For this reason it is important to set goals for ourselves, something on which we can center our hopes. It may be taking a trip, or developing some hobby, or writing a book. We may never reach our goal, but it nevertheless gives something to shoot for.

There are numerous things that tend to dim our hopes. When we experience many setbacks and disappointments, or when we are often frustrated in reaching our ideals, we may lose some of our hopes. But try to be one of those people for whom "hope swells eternal in the human breast."

CHRISTIAN HOPE

Hope is a vital power in the Christian life also. To be sure, hope is a source of comfort as we walk the last mile of the road. But it is also a great consolation to those who are left behind. Yet hope does more than that. "Every one who has this hope set on Him purifieth himself, even as He is pure," says the Apostle John.

The hope of heaven inspires men to purify their hearts and lives. This is the loftiest incentive for a Christian life. It is this hope that inspired the martyrs to face "the tyrant's brandished steel, the lion's gory mane." It is this hope that enables men to give lives of wholehearted devotion and service. And it is this hope that enables them to overcome great obstacles and difficulties. For the eye of the Christian is fixed on the future — a future that is sure and stedfast in the Person of the unchanging Christ.